Critical Acclaim for *Got, Not Got*

Got, Not Got: The A-Z of Lost Football Culture, Treasures & Pleasures

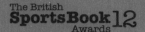

Runner-up, Best Football Book, British Sports Book Awards 2012

"A veritable Dundee cake of a book."
Danny Kelly, talkSport

"Recalling a more innocent time before Sky Sports and millionaire players, *Got, Not Got* is like a long soak in a warm bath of football nostalgia: an A-Z of memorabilia, ephemera and ill-advised haircuts."
In Demand, *Mail on Sunday Live magazine*

"The real magic is the collection and display of the illustrative material of stickers, badges, programme covers, Subbuteo figures and other ephemera. It is astonishingly thorough, well-presented, inspired and indeed had me going, 'yes, got, got, not got, forgot, never seen'."
When Saturday Comes

"A cracking book which whisks you back to a different footballing era."
Brian Reade, Mirror Football

"This memorabilia fest is a delightful reminder of what's gone from the game: 'magic sponges', Subbuteo and, er, magazines for shinpads. Such innocent times, eh?"
FourFourTwo

"The book's great fun. It's an essential if you grew up watching football in the 60s, 70s or 80s. It's a kind of football fan's catnip. Nobody can quite walk past it. They start looking at it and then realise they've got something else they should be doing 10 or 15 minutes later."
Paul Hawksbee, talkSport.

"The best book about football written in the last 20 years."
Bill Borrows, *Esquire*

"A body of work that transcends being 'just a book' by a considerable distance."
In Bed With Maradona blog

"Obviously, everybody over the
There's something
Andy

"Browsable for hours, even days, prefera   s in the
background, this is the Christmas present th   to peruse
while their neglected partner's busy basting the turkey   ing sherry...
Sit back and be blissfully reminded of adverts, food products, players, toys, kits, magazines, stickers and trends you'd long since confined to your mental attic."
Ian Plenderleith, Stay-at-Home Indie Pop blog

"I've had this for a month but haven't got round to reviewing it because it keeps disappearing. It's the sign of a good book that people repeatedly pick it up and walk away with it. A hardback collection of vintage football memorabilia that you need in your life... It's like finding your old football stickers."
James Brown, SabotageTimes.com

GOT, NOT GOT
The Lost World of Liverpool

GOT, NOT GOT
The Lost World of Liverpool

Derek Hammond & Gary Silke

Pitch Publishing Ltd
A2 Yeoman Gate
Yeoman Way
Durrington
BN13 3QZ

Email: info@pitchpublishing.co.uk
Web: www.pitchpublishing.co.uk

First published by Pitch Publishing 2014
Text © 2014 Derek Hammond and Gary Silke

13-digit ISBN: 9781909626584
Design and typesetting by Olner Pro Sport Media.
Manufacturing managed by Jellyfish Solution Ltd.
Printed and bounded in Malta by Gutenberg Press Ltd.

"The socialism I believe in isn't really politics. It's a way of living. It is humanity. I believe the only way to live and to be truly successful is by collective effort, with everyone working for each other, everyone helping each other, and everyone having a share of the rewards at the end of the day."

Bill Shankly

"We're coming in to land at Speke
My legs are feeling very weak
We've just returned from Barcelona
And now I'm going for a sauna."

John Toshack, 'Return from Spain'

A&BC

A&BC Chewing
Gum of Romford,
Essex, holds a
special place in the
hearts of millions of
big kids. Back in the
1950s, it was Douglas
Coakley (the 'C' in the
company name) who
came up with the idea of
packaging football cards
with a thin slab of chewy,
a combination which proved a natural
winner. Throughout the 1960s and
into the 1970s they produced a yearly
set of football cards, as well as other
stickers, tattoos and card series covering
everything from the Beatles to Star Trek
– and American sports and TV-related
cards bound for the US via partner
company, Topps.

Every British footballer who ever
appeared on an A&BC card was paid
a tenner image rights, and got to tell a
company agent how tall they were and
how much they cost from St Mirren, for
the blurb on the back. In 1969, George
Best and his agent tried to up the ante
to £1,000, with predictable results. The
Reds' Tommy Smith also reckoned his
rocklike features were worth more, but
after a phone call explaining that the
fee was no indication of star stature,
and a useful little earner for many of
the checklist's lesser lights, 'The Anfield
Iron' signed up with good grace.

Unfortunately, in
1974, A&BC lost a
long-simmering legal
battle and was taken
over by Topps-
Bazooka. End of
story.

But, for some
reason, it isn't
easy to put out of
your mind stray memories of
football's long-lost people and
places, the youthful obsessions
and outdated rituals that
seemed so important back in
the day – and, in a strange way, still do.
It might be a name on an email that you
immediately associate with a recoloured
kit on a card, and think: "Not got." Or
just a vacant moment
when you're driving
at 80mph down the
M6, when you find
yourself wondering…
whatever happened
to Alun Evans?

It isn't everyone
who could possibly
understand.

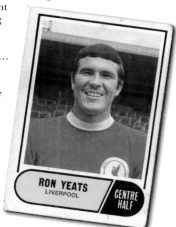

*Ron Yeats: An easy
mistake to make for any
mustard-keen seven-year-
old footy card collector.*

ACTION MEN

They don't make boys' toys like Action Man any more.

Kids aren't interested in peering through the back of a plastic doll's head and into his 'Eagle Eye' when the maximum thrill available is a slightly blurred view of the back garden. And as for realistic hair and gripping hands... they tend to pale into insignificance next to the Xbox's 3-D virtual world, where it's perfectly possible to drop in on

Inaction Man: Great at getting blown up, not so hot at close control or diving headers.

Berlin in 1945 or Pluto in the year 4567, shredding Nazis and aliens alike with a sonic fire ray akin to a red-mist glare from Jimmy Case.

They'd call Action Man un-PC now – an eight-inch multi-skilled terrorist who thought nothing of changing out of his Nazi Stormtrooper uniform into that of a Navy frogman, a Canadian Mountie or an astronaut. And so into his Liverpool kit for a kickaround with your sister's Barbie in goal.

Unfortunately, that's when our vicious little accomplice became a complete bore. Whether you had one Action Man or 22, there just wasn't a game you could base around his non-existent ball skills. The specific types of 'action' mastered by 'the movable fighting man' were limited to bending at the joints and being blown into the air. There was only so much fun you could have dressing a doll in football kit, especially as it exposed his shattered-looking kneecaps. The final straw was

the orthopaedic stand which he needed to balance on one leg, hovering over the ball in a sorry personification of inaction.

Because most Action Man enthusiasts kept their figures strictly military, the scarcity value of the football range has more recently seen eBay prices soaring. Original 1960s Liverpool kits regularly sell on the auction site for over £250, and the red Action Man team badge given away with the original kit pack can sell for over fifty quid alone.

If only you'd kept them, Action Man's two-inch-long red socks could now pay for a decent night out.

Try painting a 'Crown Paints' logo over those tricky pinstripes on a bloke who's two inches tall.

AIRFIX

Ever since 1955, when they released their 1/72 Spitfire model kit, Airfix had been satisfying little boys' unquenchable thirst for recreating World War II.

You could paint up a boxful of Commandos or Desert Rats and painstakingly put together a Hampden bomber, though how you were supposed to stop the 'cement' from clouding up the glass canopy of the cockpit was anyone's guess.

Even more satisfying than endless war was the 1/32nd scale Airfix Sports Series of Airfix Footballers – your chance to ditch khaki and grey for the far more exciting football colours of red, white and black, and maybe even a few of those other oppo colours like sky blue and canary yellow.

Up until the mid-Seventies it wasn't too much trouble recreating miniature versions of the kits of the day; but things got a lot trickier after that time.

Go on, you try painting an Umbro badge, Adidas sleeve stripes or a

microscopic 'Hitachi' logo on a bloke who's just over two inches tall.

Long boring Sunday afternoons were the perfect time for creating a pair of Umbro shorts, complete with the manufacturer's diamond and club crest on the front – right up until the double misery of *Last of the Summer Wine* and the parental enquiry: "Have you got any homework, son?" reminded you that Monday morning was nearly upon us once again.

Thanks to eBay you can still get that distinctive box through the post with England vs. Germany on the front. Old habits, like old enemies, die hard. And if you've got a steady hand and a couple of hundred hours on your hands, there's no more satisfying way to waste your time.

THE ROSETTE

In the olden days, British males over the age of six were only permitted to wear brown, grey, greeny-brown, browny-green or, in moments of extreme flamboyance, navy.

If a chap had worn a football jersey anywhere other than on a football field he might well have been assumed to have taken leave of his senses, and arrested for causing a breach of the peace.

And the same applied to sporting any item of apparel other than a school blazer in a primary colour. Red socks and yellow waistcoats, for example, were only ever sported by show-offs, buffoons and variety acts.

So how to let it be known which side you were supporting in the big Cup game on Saturday? That's where red-and-white rosettes came in: they were the acceptable face of partisanship in more restrained times.

You don't get them any more.

LIVERPOOL
FOOTBALL CLUB
CUP FINAL 1977.

Liverpool
Rome 77

LIVERPOOL
EUROPEAN CUP WINNERS
& LEAGUE CHAMPS

LIVERPOOL F.C.
CHAMPIONS OF CHAMPIONS
LEAGUE CHAMPIONS 1976
U.E.F.A. CUP WINNERS 1976

THE SCRAPPER

In the six-million-year interval between man first walking upright and the invention of the 24-hour kids' TV channel, the PlayStation, the Xbox, the Wii and the DS, kids were faced with a bit of a challenge. How to fill all those long, boring hours before it was time to blow their candles out? It was merely hundreds of years ago when the penny finally dropped, and pastimes such as needlepoint, pressing wild flowers and making your own scrapbook at last began to gain popularity.

Most young football fans had a go at assembling scraps devoted to their football team, but few persisted for very long. The first page of every scrapbook is filled, the last page hardly ever. After a few weeks, cutting your club's match reports and photos out of the paper tended to become a chore, enabling you to later track the ever-decreasing degree of care with which they were Gloyed on to the coarse pages. And then there was that final time you jumped the gun and Dad found a comedy hole in the back of his *Sunday Express* before he'd finished with it.

My Back Pages: lots of crinkly paper, yellowing glue and spent, sticky-free Sellotape.

CHARLES BUCHAN'S FOOTBALL MONTHLY

It was the world's first monthly football magazine, unleashed on Britain's thrill-starved youth in September 1951 – and, despite missing the start of his debut season, *Charlie Buchan's* proved an instant hit.

Here, at last, was some colour to brighten the grey post-war landscape covered by the monochrome grown-up media. At least, bright pastel colours were daubed over black-and-white photos to vivid effect. And, in an era when kids were only expected to speak when spoken to, Charlie undid the top button of his sports jacket and did his best to address the herbets.

Even from the standpoint of sixty years on, the magazine's format is strikingly familiar, suggesting Charlie's editorial team got it pretty much right first time. There's analysis and tips from ex-pros and other enthusiastic scribblers; there's page-size posters for the bedroom wall, and interviews with players who aren't allowed to say anything.

Thumbing now through Charlie's back pages, he provides a unique window into an unrecognisable world of side partings and V-neck shirts, of rugby boots and weirdly recoloured violet irises.

From the magazine's perspective, football was steering into choppy waters when Buchan himself died in 1960, leaving the *Monthly* rudderless in the face of tidal changes such as footballers demanding a minimum wage, and suddenly not all agreeing to sport leather hair.

Although it limped on until 1974, *Football Monthly* never stood a chance against the new generation of marginally more readable comics and magazines put together by people who had heard of the Rolling Stones. *Shoot! Goal.* Mud, even, eventually.

If it proves anything, it's probably that in retrospect every age seems like a Golden Age, provided you were ten.

THE CIGARETTE CARD

In the age of No Smoking – when anyone who fancies a tab is forced to stand outside their office in all weathers, and even crowd into a ramshackle lean-to hurriedly added twixt bar and beer garden – it won't be long until kids don't even recognise the reference to a good old-fashioned gasper, already obscured by the slick, sad euphemism of 'candy stick'.

The sweetie cigarette will soon be no more, like Terry Mac's perm, mud and lunchtime Merseybeat at The Cavern.

Back in the day, however, they were clearly the best option for L-plate smokers, both in terms of their unique, chalky-sweet flavour and cunning authenticity, courtesy of a dab of pink

cult of the cigarette card proper will soon be nothing but a memory clung to by a disappearing breed of oldsters.

No, not the stout men who smoked for England during the war only to be stamped out underfoot in the fallout from NHS cost-cutting exercises determined to make everyone live to 200. But us, the jammy-faced kids who remember the well-thumbed contents of Granddad's hand-me-down baccy tin.

We posed manfully with a sugary cig dangling from our lips,

fooling absolutely everybody.

food colouring on the burning 'hot' end. And they came with a football card, too, if you were lucky – or a fat cricketer or lady tennis player if the dreaded mixed-sports set was in season.

Barratt's and Bassett's packs of sweet cigarettes were a throwback to the cigarette cards that had died out in the war; but we never realised that at the time. We were too busy posing manfully with our sugary cig dangling from our lips, fooling absolutely everybody.

Sweetie cigarette cards are already an obscurity to kids aged under 20 or 30. And the original pre-war mass

Redder than thou: Tom models a pair of fantastic prototype crimson Hummels.

13

ROY OF THE ROVERS

You don't have to be a genius to work out which team the legendary (well okay, fictional) Melchester Rovers were based on – or at least which team Roy Race's invincible club side inevitably became most closely associated with back in the sunny 1970s and 80s.

Clue: they played in all red with sexy, dynamic yellow flourishes.

Clue: they won the League pretty much every year, except in the odd season when Roy was having marital problems with Penny, and the storyline more closely resembled a soap opera, what with Rovers losing the odd match to unfeasible underdogs.

Clue: they won the FA Cup pretty much every season, too.

Clue: and then off they went around the world in the close season, taking on evil Bond baddies' pet

football teams and being forced to play cricket against crazed billionaires' pet village teams. And, oh yes…

Clue: they won in Europe pretty much every season, too – usually against

Why, some of those storylines were bordering on the ridiculous. Nothing at all to do with the precious original concept of a sturdy club side from the north of England wiping the floor with the oppo

In the European Cup, Roy and his Rovers took on

evil Bond baddies' private football teams.

sneaky foreign communist fascist cheaty types like Dynamo Zarkovia and Borussia Goebbelsgladbach.

We're not counting those very late strips where Roy got shot and had a helicopter accident and had his leg amputated, mind.

every week, winning a rerun of World War II every summer and still having time to guest alongside the friendly natives of Juju Island against scarred chip-on-shoulder megalomaniacs threatening the stability of football-mad Polynesia.

For 'Roy' read 'Kenny', for 'Melchester' read 'Liverpool'…

15

THE TENACIOUS WARRIOR

1966 is remembered for glorious, golden images of a grinning, red-shirted Bobby Moore, carried on his team-mates' shoulders, holding aloft the Jules Rimet trophy. However, from a non-English point of view, the tournament saw world football reach a nadir of cynical foul play. It's known across the footballing globe as the 'Dirty World Cup'.

It was a time when defenders appeared to have free rein to hoof lumps out of strikers, who were given virtually no protection from referees. Full-backs had grown tired of being made to look like monkeys by the likes of Stanley Matthews and had discovered that there was more than one way to stop a tricky winger.

The nominated hard man of each club was almost as celebrated as the star strikers they sought to

Tom tackled determinedly. He was a brave and loyal servant who received the MBE for services to football.

bruise: Ron 'Chopper' Harris of Chelsea; Man U's Nobby Stiles; Leeds United's Norman 'Bites Yer Legs' Hunter (and a few more besides); Tottenham's Dave Mackay...

In other words, players you loved to hate – unless they happened to be on your side, in which case there was often room for a small amount of give-and-take. A healthy alternative perspective on their tendency towards ultraviolence.

Take Tommy Smith, for example: he was a warrior, a loyal servant for 16 years and 623 games; a man you'd want to go to war with, but certainly not against.

Oppo fans were often incensed by his high spirits, his tenacious, uncompromising tackling and never-say-die attitude, which was totally different in nature to the common yobs previously mentioned.

There seemed to be a complicit understanding between a good old-fashioned hard man and referee whereby no one could be booked in the opening five minutes of a game. He was allowed one free, 'welcoming' clog on an opposing forward's calf, 'just to let them know I'm here'.

The second, Achilles-crunching challenge might warrant a brief word of warning from the ref. The third might occasionally earn a booking, at which the defender would present a picture of outraged innocence.

By this stage, the talented striker had completely lost:

1 – stomach for the contest; or,
2 – all feeling below the waist.

And the job was a good 'un.

Identity parade: Nowadays, fans have moved on from all-over badges to all-over Liverpool tattoos.

COFFER BADGES

Back in the day, no self-respecting teenager would be seen at a football match or out on the town without a denim jacket rendered almost invisible under the weight of Coffer enamel badges, spilling out over the full area of their scarf and bobble hat, while sew-on patches tumbled all the way down the back and arms.

Liverpool
Ace in the Pack!
Liverpool Rule OK!

The very sight of all these vintage badges is almost enough to make anybody start yearning for a proper stripy scarf weighing anything upwards of three or four pounds – while the messages they carry recalls nagging mum to stitch as many patches as humanly possible on to your parka sleeves and Army Surplus schoolbag.

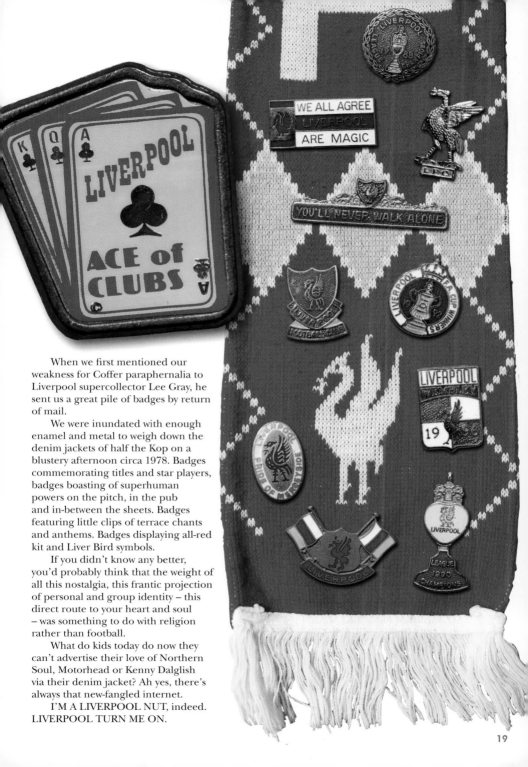

When we first mentioned our weakness for Coffer paraphernalia to Liverpool supercollector Lee Gray, he sent us a great pile of badges by return of mail.

We were inundated with enough enamel and metal to weigh down the denim jackets of half the Kop on a blustery afternoon circa 1978. Badges commemorating titles and star players, badges boasting of superhuman powers on the pitch, in the pub and in-between the sheets. Badges featuring little clips of terrace chants and anthems. Badges displaying all-red kit and Liver Bird symbols.

If you didn't know any better, you'd probably think that the weight of all this nostalgia, this frantic projection of personal and group identity – this direct route to your heart and soul – was something to do with religion rather than football.

What do kids today do now they can't advertise their love of Northern Soul, Motorhead or Kenny Dalglish via their denim jacket? Ah yes, there's always that new-fangled internet.

I'M A LIVERPOOL NUT, indeed. LIVERPOOL TURN ME ON.

Cotton is perfectly soft and natural,
alternately warm and cool,
and shrink resistant.

COTTON

It's the sensual associations that come bundled with cotton that make it such a rich source of minor, if largely subconscious, pleasure.

Ahh, the smell of a new cotton T-shirt being pulled on over your head on a Friday night. The slow fade of a favourite shirt, laundered a hundred times by your mum. Cotton next to the skin – warm against the winter cold, cool in summer... the pure smell of plain red, a simple Liver Bird crest, and no other labels or logos smelling of a modern attempt to cash in.

In 150 years, the only negatives against cotton were an association with hippie cheesecloth and, ah yes, the institutionalised horrors of the slave trade.

Cotton isn't just perfect for clothes because it's easy to take care of and to wash. It's soft because it's made out of perfectly natural fluff. And it's cheap because the fluff grows on trees.

And so some tiresome bean counter inevitably decided to put about the idea that cotton is altogether second rate. Wear it for sports and it apparently now soaks up sweat in a way that you wouldn't want it to be soaked up. Cotton isn't stretchy enough, and it needs ironing, unlike a certain artificial wonder-fabric. They even tried to convince us that shell-suit bottoms were cooler and more comfortable than jeans.

Now, it just so happens that while cotton is cheap, polyester is cheaper. So much cheaper, it's practically free.

Polyester is an artificial plastic made from the acids and alcohol produced when you torch petroleum – in other words, from exhaust fumes.

Polyester is hard-wearing primarily because it's hard. It's rough to the touch, keeps you cold in winter and hot in summer. Wear it in summer, or for sports, and it will make you smell like you've been dead for a week.

Bring back cotton football shirts!

CLUBCALL

Back in the Eighties and Nineties, it was the sheer unavailability of up-to-the-minute club information that made it so tantalising. So valuable.

You wouldn't want everyone else to know that David Johnson had a hammy, would you? – not if you were still thinking he might be playing on Saturday. You wouldn't want to miss what 'Wantaway' Ian Callaghan had allegedly denied this morning – or boss Bob Paisley's counter-denials of any new ace winger rumours. Ahh, the rumours...

The Clubcall service came as a blessing for all fans – especially those exiled from local news and those trapped at work with the benefit of a free phone to avoid the disgraceful premium call rates.

At the end of the line – literally – was a local newspaper stringer (or at least an Ansafone recording of him) summing up

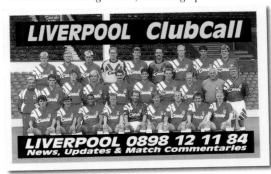

You Got My Number (Why Don't You Use It?): If you wanna wanna wanna wanna wanna have someone to talk to...

back-page stories from yesterday's evening paper and this morning's tabs. To deliver value for money, he also used to make up juicy filler on the spot, and read it out. S-l-o-w-l-y.

"Hello... and it's a big... Liverpule... welcome... to your exclusive... front-line... Clubcall service for... Liverpule... Football... Club.

"Listen to... Clubcall... for all the latest... news... and... information..."

Because we were paying by the second.

21

141

142

Led the club to the Leagu...
ship and UEFA Cup win...
captain. Wing-half signe...
and a paid performer since
...ation 1966. You...
England cap.

87 DAVID FAIRCLOUGH

192 KEVIN KEEGAN

THE WONDERFUL WORLD OF SOCCER STARS

How many sets of football cards and stickers do you reckon might have been pushed out into the UK market to mark the occasion of the 1966 World Cup? Ten? Twenty? The answer, you might be surprised to hear, is none. Not a one. Zero.

In recent years a limited test production of A&BC World Cup stamps has emerged, but these are priceless rarities that had no real impact. Even though pocket-size cardboard football cards had been successfully covering the domestic game since the end of the '50s, and European and South American manufacturers had produced trailblazing sticker books for the 1962 finals, it simply didn't occur to anyone to build on these trends.

It was only when England secured Monsieur Rimet's small gold trophy that the enthusiasm really rocketed, kick-starting the British football industry in the stands, in the shops and in sticker albums up and down the country.

In the second half of the '60s, playgrounds rocked to the tribal rhythm of "Got, got, got, got, not got" as kids flicked through their teetering piles in search of that elusive Chris Lawler, perfectly willing to exchange 200 swaps to fill in the one remaining square left on their checklist.

If us Brits were slow off the mark seeing the possibilities in the market for cards and World Cups, it took even longer to get the ball rolling on the Euro-led non-sticky sticker front.

In 1967, FKS's 'Wonderful World of Soccer Stars' rolled into limited, regional production, reflecting a Golden Age when all you needed to start up business in the football sticker market was a picture deal with an agency – no worries if the images were a season or two out of

Founded: 1892. Ground: Anfield. Manager: Bob Paisley. League Champions: 1901, 1906, 1922, 1923, 1947, 1964, 1966, 1973, 1976. F. A. Cup: 1965, 1974. UEFA Cup: 1973, 1976.

LIVERPOOL

IAN CALLAGHAN

JIMMY CASE

RAY CLEMENCE

PETER CORMACK

DAVID FAIRCLOUGH

BRIAN HALL

PICTUR...

IAN ST. JOHN

GEOFF STRONG

PETER THOMPSON

RON YEATS

Founded: 1892. Ground: Anfield. Ma...
Bob Paisley. League Champions: 1901...
1922, 1923, 1947, 1964, 1966, 1973. F.A...
1965, 1974. UEFA Cup: 1973.

date, that's what retouching brushes are for – and a distribution deal around the corner shops of Britain.

The idea took off, and 1968 saw the first widely available sticker set, largely repeating the previous year's mugshot efforts. The following season's largely accidental mix of action shots and head-and-shoulders upped the excitement greatly and has rarely been bettered, still offering a real window into the Wonderful, and sadly Lost World of Football in the Sixties.

The business model was clear. Give any football-mad child a packet of (not really very accurately titled) stickers, an album and a pot of Gloy gum, let him stick his first sticker into the allotted slot, surrounded by another dozen blank spaces taunting him, and let nature take its course...

RAY CLEMENCE

PETER COR...

SOCCER STARS '76 '77

...ORD...

AMP ALBUM

LIVERPOOL

Founded: 1892
Ground: Anfield Road
Manager: Bill Shankly
League Champions: 1901, 1906,
1922, 1923, 1947, 1964, 1966; F.A.
Cup: 1965.

IAN CALLAGHAN

RAY CLEMENCE

...ANTSHIRE

BOBBY GRAHAM

BRIAN HALL

STEVE HEIGHWAY

EML...

CHRIS LAWLER

ALEC LINDSAY

LARRY LLOYD

23

...OHN M...

FANZINES

Following on from the Seventies' music-led revolutions in DIY publishing, including Liverpool's legendary *The End*, it took a while for football to catch up, but eventually fans took to their cranky old typewriters, hunting and pecking and ker-chinging out their frustrations, and learning all-new reprographic skills along the way.

They were tired of hearing 'The Fans' View' expressed second hand in the media, where the final word, the final edit, was always predictably happy and safe. Before the 1980s, every word written about football came from an industry perspective – tapped out by writers who were paid by newspapers, magazines, television companies or club programmes, which were in turn reliant on the FA, the League or the clubs themselves.

Jokes at our own expense, better jokes at Everton's expense, stories of away trips, pubs and pies.

WHEN SUNDAY COMES
ISSUE 3 OCT 1988 40 PENCE

IANWHO?

LIVERPOOL SIGN UNKNOWN WELSH DUSTMAN
INSIDE: Loads more out of date stuff

It's a tough job, running the back page of a local paper without access to news information, player interviews or pictures.

No such problem for the first wave of fanzine rebels, who offered an all-new diet of uncensored opinion cut with terrace humour, finally putting the majority view of 20,000 regulars above the handful of professionals and hired hands – the chairman, the players, the manager, the gentlemen of the press box – who were just passing through.

Suddenly your familiar old programme seller had a bit of competition on the streets from titles like: *Through the Wind and Rain*, and *When Sunday Comes,*

No matter if they were presented under headlines written using felt-pen, Letraset or John Bull Printing Outfit No. 7: here, for the very first time in print, were negative as well as positive views on our beloved clubs and teams, jokes at our own expense, better jokes at Everton's expense, album and gig reviews, stories of away trips, pubs and pies… always pies.

And, somewhere along the way, we discovered it wasn't just the fans in our corner of our ground who felt the same way about all-seater stadiums and ID cards, about the wreckers who came to football to chuck bananas and seats on the pitch, and the wreckers who came bearing calculators. And pies.

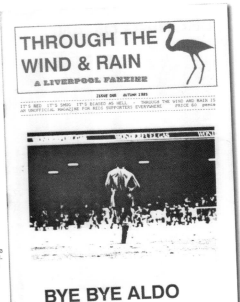

THROUGH THE WIND & RAIN
A LIVERPOOL FANZINE

ISSUE ONE AUTUMN 1985

IT'S RED IT'S SMUG IT'S BIASED AS HELL – THROUGH THE WIND AND RAIN IS AN UNOFFICIAL MAGAZINE FOR REDS SUPPORTERS EVERYWHERE PRICE 60 pence

BYE BYE ALDO

When Skies Are Red: Black-and-white and Red all over…

THE FOOTBALL CARD ENGINE

Here's how to transform your humble pushbike into a revved-up, throbbing beast of a motorcycle, all too easy to mistake for a 750cc Norton Commando (provided you're only listening rather than looking).

All you need is:

1 – One giant pile of football cards;
2 – Two clothes pegs;
3 – An anti-social desire to terrorise your neighbours like those cool Hells Angels you've seen on *Nationwide*; and,
4 – A tragic disregard for your future financial security.

If you've got a teetering pile of cards, it naturally follows that you've got an even bigger pile of swaps, collected up over weeks of frustration while searching for the two or three you need for the set.

We recommend you use an Alec Lindsay 'blue-back' from Topps' 1976-77 series. He's got a nice woody thrum.

ALEC LINDSAY

LIVERPOOL

PHIL THOMPSON

Transform your pushbike into a Hells Angel's Norton Commando
with Alec Lindsay's woody thrum.

All you have to do is use the pegs to secure the cards on to your bike frame so they stick a little way into the spokes. Then push off, taking note of the unusual sensation of slight resistance as you wobble down the gutter, turning heads with a guttural, engine-like *Vrrrrrrrrrrrp*.

This way, in one afternoon you might easily burn through £100s worth of future sought-after collectables at 21st-century prices. But what the heck. You're only young once, eh?

IAN CALLAGHAN

Boot Boys: Boss Bill Shankly, Bob Paisley, Ronnie Moran, Joe Fagan and Reuben Bennett.

THE BOOT ROOM

It is nice to think that the discussions and decisions that turned Liverpool FC into the overwhelming force of the Seventies and Eighties didn't take place in a gleaming, opulent boardroom over highly polished mahogany, but in a dingy hideaway in Anfield's main stand – designed as a place to store boots.

Bill Shankly, Reuben Bennett, Bob Paisley, Tom Saunders and Joe Fagan were the original members of this collective, and Fagan noted:

"In time it would become furnished with luxuries like a rickety old table and a couple of plastic chairs, a tatty piece of carpet on the floor and a calendar on a wall that would later be adorned with photographs, ripped from newspapers, of topless models..."

The original Boot Room was in the best traditions of the British bloke's shed.

It was in the best traditions of the British bloke's shed.

When Shankly arrived in December 1959, Liverpool were a struggling second division outfit in serious decline. This was mirrored in the facilities at Anfield, which was in poor shape, and the Melwood training ground which was even worse. Shankly and his backroom staff spent the first day of his new job picking the stones and broken glass off the training pitches. Having literally picked Liverpool up from the ground, Shankly enjoyed 15 years littered with silverware, and when he retired the dynasty pushed forward Bob Paisley in his place, who went on to win even more trophies, and then Joe Fagan took his turn.

In the meantime, names like Ronnie Moran, Roy Evans and Kenny Dalglish had done their time among the dubbin and studs, carrying on the tradition.

Eventually, the Boot Room was demolished to accommodate a new media centre during Graeme Souness's time as manager in the early Nineties. Liverpool haven't won a League title since.

THE FOOTBALL LEAGUE REVIEW

Run from the back bedroom of secretary Alan Hardaker's Blackpool bungalow, the Football League was devoted to showing everyone what a big, happy family their 92-member club was. The *Football League Review* was a feelgood customer mag, given away free inside club programmes, where it bolstered many four- or eight-page lower-league efforts. The *FLR* was conspicuous in its absence from several larger League grounds, where power brokers were already wary of growing League influence.

Football League Revie

THE OFFICIAL JOURNAL OF THE FOOTBALL LEAGUE

League
FOOTBALL
5p

The Review was 5 pence 'when bought separately'; which is to say never.

However, in stark comparison to the petty politicking backstabbing golf-clubbing small-minded scrap-metal merchant football-club owners of the 1970s, fans dug the freebies to bits – especially if Brian Hall featured on the cover.

The *Review* was 5 pence 'when bought separately'; which is to say never. It was full of behind-the-scenes peeks at the day-to-day running of all the League clubs, an article on the bootroom at

HASTILY RECOLOURED KIT

Although there was a lot less movement in the transfer market than today, the photo agencies that supplied the football card and sticker manufacturers in the Sixties and Seventies were rarely bang up-to-date.

Cue the burning of midnight oil as heads were snipped off and reapplied to new teammates' bodies, and old shirts hastily penned with new colours.

You've got to love bodge jobs like this Sixties FKS sticker of Jack Whitham playing for Sheff Wed – then coincidentally adopting exactly the same pose in exactly the same spot in Reds kit a year later.

FKS albums even carried a straight-faced 'guarantee': 'In order to maintain authenticity, some of the players have been photographed in clothing which is not necessarily their official club colours'.

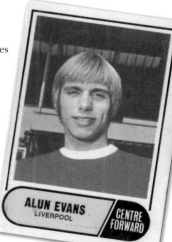

ALUN EVANS
LIVERPOOL
CENTRE FORWARD

Alun Evans of Liverpool. Not Wolves, honest guv.

Barrow being just as likely as a visit to the Arsenal trophy room. Then and now, its allure was almost entirely down to staff photographer Peter Robinson, who spent whole seasons travelling around snapping mascots at Mansfield and tea-ladies in Tranmere, thinking up ever more unusual formations for his teamgroups.

"I was conscious that I was different when I talked with other photographers at games," he told *When Saturday Comes*. Robinson never missed an angle, an expression, an oddity or a location, showing more interest in football culture than the game itself. "I felt that you didn't just have to start photographing when the ref blew his whistle. I was interested in the whole build-up to the game."

ITV SUNDAY AFTERNOON FOOTBALL

Doo-doodle doo-doodle doo-doo doo-doo-doo...

Remember the theme tune from Sunday afternoon football on Granada – the *Kick Off* programme, presented by Gerald Sinstadt? It must bring back millions of mass memories of roast beef and Yorkshire puddings for the endless trail of nostalgic types who give it a spin on YouTube.

There was little room for manoeuvre in the editing suite, back then. The main game, however incident-packed or dull, ran for fifteen minutes up to a half-time ad break,

Remember the theme tune from Granada's Kick Off?

followed by another quarter of an hour for the second half.

Part three brought fifteen minutes of a game from another ITV region, maybe yours. Hugh Johns was the smoky voice of ATV's *Star Soccer*, Tyne Tees was Kenneth Wolstenholme on *Shoot*, while LWT's *The Big Match* was fronted by Brian Moore...

After part four's brief highlights of another game – maybe Norwich or Ipswich from Anglia's *Match of the Week* with Gerry Harrison – and a round-up of results, the weekend seemed almost over.

Dozens of games went untelevised every weekend and that's why seeing your team was so special. With perhaps only a handful of TV appearances in a lean year, the novelty never wore off.

Which is why Reds fans lucky enough to work from home are always sneaking off to YouTube to find clips from the actual matches, as well as the great old pop-art titles.

Doo-doodle doo-doodle doo-doo doo-doo-doo...

Afternoon Delight: Roast beef, Yorkshire pud and Gerald Sinstadt.

CHAMPAGNE MAGNUM

League Championship 1972-73, 75-76, 76-77, 78-79, 79-80, 81-82, 82-83, 83-84, 85-86, 87-88; European Cup 1977, 1978, 1981, 1984; UEFA Cup 1973, 1976; FA Cup 1974, 1986, 1989…

GRAEME SOUNESS

DAVID JOHNSON

The stats alone are immense, but they don't quite convey the awesome sight of Liverpool at Anfield, attacking the Kop with all the insistence of waves crashing on the shore. As for how and why, Liverpool's overpowering period of success was at least partly due to their magnificent

Johnson, and with Steve Heighway's 'Mexican Bandit' on the bench, they had a yard-and-a-half of bristles between them in a team look that could have been planned to steal trophies.

'Fu Manchu', 'Sergeant Pepper', 'Magnum', 'McDermott'.

line-up of moustaches.

What bare-lipped opposition wouldn't feel a little bit intimidated by such a manly array of facial furniture: Bruce Grobbelaar's 'Fu Manchu'; Mark Lawrenson's 'Sergeant Pepper'; Graeme Souness's 'Magnum'; Terry McDermott's 'McDermott'.

Backed up by Ian Rush, John Aldridge, Alan Kennedy, Jimmy Case, David

TERRY McDERMOTT

LEAGUE LADDERS

Wahey! Liverpool top of the League!

But there was more to your youthful flights of League Ladder-related fantasy than mere self-centred feelgood relish. There was also the bottom of Scottish League Division Two to consider (or maybe, if you were feeling generous, the bottom of the Fourth Division, and the basement trapdoor beckoning into non-League Hell). That's where a good old English emotion known as *schadenfreude* took over – and where you found clustered the likes of Everton, Manchester United, Leeds United and Tranmere Rovers. Not to mention every other side that had put one over on the Reds in the past three seasons.

Gifted to us in the build-up to the season's big kick-off by *Shoot!* or *Roy of the Rovers* or one of the old-school shoot-'em-up comics such as *Lion* or *Valiant*, the empty league ladders came first, closely followed over a number of weeks with the small cardboard team tabs designed to be poked into their ever-changing slot in the scheme of things.

In the days before computers, even before Teletext, the appeal of being able to stare at the league table was considerable. But, after the third or fourth week, updating your league ladders became a bit too much like hard work.

And that's when you could see what it would look like if East Fife were somehow suddenly transported to second in the League behind its natural eternal leaders. Ha! Swansea in the First Division, and Burnley in the Fourth! And all those lesser Lancashire clubs mysteriously close to going out of business – pointless, crowdless and hopeless, as God intended.

LIVERPOOL

Ground: Anfield Road, Liverpool 4.

Team tab: Cut out and keep, and collect the whole set of 92!

32

1st DIVISION

English League
SOCCER WEEKLY

SHOOT/GOAL

1st DIVISION

1	LIVERPOOL
2	ARSENAL
3	QUEEN'S P.R.
4	TOTTENHAM
5	IPSWICH
6	SUNDERLAND
7	WEST HAM
8	ASTON VILLA
9	MANCHESTER C.
10	STOKE
11	LEICESTER
12	NEWCASTLE
13	LEEDS
14	NORWICH
15	BIRMINGHAM
16	COVENTRY
17	MIDDLESBRO'
18	WOLVES
19	DERBY
20	WEST BROM
21	EVERTON
22	MANCHESTER U.

2nd DIVISION

1
2
3
4
5
6
7
8
9
10
11
12
13
14
15
16
17
18
19
20
21
22

all there is to k... with SHOOT.
SHOOT will ...ked with inform...
...s and feature... every aspect...
... and colour

...bby Styles, some...
...Training—in full...
...ry of the Europe...
...oore writes the

H LEAGUE
2nd DIV

1	ST. JOHNSTONE
2	E. STIRLING
3	MORTON
4	HAMILTON A.
5	STRANRAER
6	ARBROATH
7	ALBION R.
8	COWDENBEATH
9	ALLOA
10	STIRLING A.
11	EAST FIFE
12	DUMBARTON
13	AYR U.
14	QUEEN'S PARK
15	MONTROSE

PROGRESS CHART...

Position	1976						1977			
	AUG	SEP	OCT	NOV	DEC	JAN	FEB	MAR	AP
	14 21 28	4 11 18 25	2 9 16 23 30	6 13 20 27	4 11 18 25	1 8 15 22 29	5 12 19 26	5 12 19 26	2 9

33

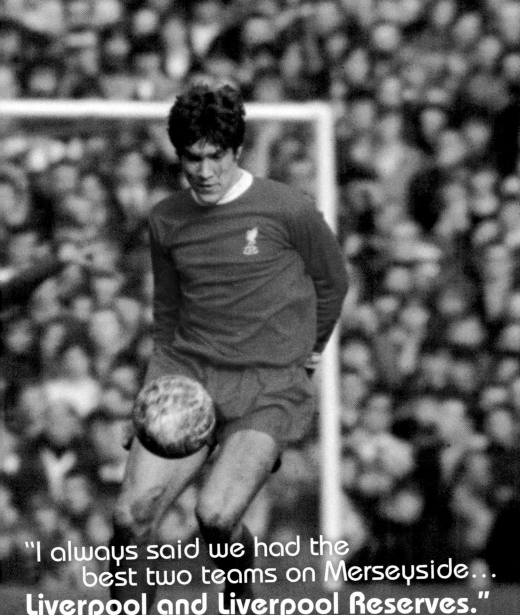

"I always said we had the
best two teams on Merseyside...
Liverpool and Liverpool Reserves."

Bill Shankly

OL FOOTBALL CLUB
F.A.
CHALLENGE CUP
AT ANFIELD
& Details as Announced
ON KOP END ONLY
IOR CITIZEN/JUNIOR
Ticket & Match Information
-260 9999
NO
THIS PORTION

LIVERPOOL FOOTBALL CLUB

Carlsberg LIVERPOOL

LIVERPOOL v. NORWICH CITY
AT ANFIELD
DATE AS ANNOUNCED
HOME SUPPORTERS ONLY
SPION KOP END
ADULT
ADMISSION
£8.00 inc. VAT
RETAINED
NO 3509
P. B. Robinson

ANFIELD ROAD 61-64 65-66
ORS ONLY
road stand
Police 5
4
to th
Foo

LIVERPOOL
FOOTBALL CLUB
LIVERPOOL FOOTBALL CLUB EST. 1892
MAIN STAND
Season Ticket 1994/95

LIVERPOOL FOOTBALL CLUB
F.A. Challenge Cup-tie
At Anfield
Ticket and Match Information
051-260 9999 (24 hour service)
GROUND TICKET
SPION KOP
NO 10541
This portion to be retained

Aston Villa Football Club Ltd.   NO 11827
F.A. Cup   SEMI-FINAL
AT VILLA PARK, BIRMINGHAM
SATURDAY, 27th, MARCH 1965   Kick-off 3.0 p.m.
LIVERPOOL v. CHELSEA
Standing Enclosure 7/6
Entrance Door   F   TRINITY ROAD
Aston Villa F.C. Ltd.
Ticket is issued subject to the Bye-laws and Regulations of the Football Association

Official Sponsor
Candy
L.F.C.
LIVERPOOL
FOOTBALL CLUB
HOME SUPPORTERS
AREA ONLY
SPION KOP
ADULT
ONLY
CUP COMPETITION
TIE AT ANFIELD
TICKET SERIES 'D'
For date & other details see national & local press
THIS PORTION TO BE RETAINED
This ticket is available for this match on whatever date it may be played
NO 3454
P. B. Robinson
General Secretary

NSFIELD TOWN F.C. LTD
FIELD MILL MANSFIELD
CUP SIXTH ROUND
day 8th Mar. 1969
KICK OFF 3 p.m.
VERSUS
ster or L'pool
OSURE 8/-
no ticket exchanged
nor money refunded
J. D. Eaton
SECRETARY
THIS PORTION TO BE RETAINED

ENTRANC
A
SEE PLAN
ON BACK
You are re
quested to
take up your
position thirty
minutes before
Kick-off

KEMLYN ROAD
77 - 84

kemlyn road

Turnstile Nos. 3-10

WALTON BRECK ROAD

11-20

development association

34-37

LIVERPOOL FOOTBALL CLUB
U.E.F.A. CUP COMPETITION
QUARTER FINAL, 2nd LEG AT ANFIELD.
LIVERPOOL F.C.
VERSUS
GENOA 1893
(ITALY)
WEDNESDAY, 18th MARCH, 1992
KICK OFF 7.10 pm
HOME SUPPORTERS: ADULT ONLY
SPION KOP
No. 6584
THIS PORTION TO BE RETAINED

OFFICIAL SPONSOR
Candy

LIVERPOOL FOOTBALL CLUB
F.A. Challenge Cup-tie
At Anfield
Ticket and Match information
051-260 9999 (24 hour service)
GROUND TICKET
SPION KOP
No. 214

Liverpool Football Club
MAIN STAND
1980 1981
REGISTERED

COVENTRY CITY FOOTBALL CLUB LTD.
Highfield Road Stadium, Coventry
Football League Division 1
COVENTRY CITY
versus
LIVERPOOL
SAT., 30th NOVEMBER, 1974, at 3.00 p.m.
£1.20
E. Plumley
General Secretary
(Plan of Ground Overleaf)

ROW
X
SEAT
8

LIVERPOOL
FOOTBALL CLUB
LIVERPOOL
FOOTBALL CLUB
EST. 1892
MAIN STAND
Season
Ticket
1995/96

LIVERPOOL FOOTBALL CLUB
SEASON 1989/90
No.
SPARE
VOUCHER 20
KEMLYN ROAD STAND

MIRRORCARDS

Back in the sunny 1971-72 season, the *Daily Mirror* was kind enough to give away a set of football cards featuring teamgroups of all 92 League clubs, plus the four Home International squads. The cards could be collected up and stuck on a large wallchart entitled 'Bobby Moore's Gallery of Soccer Sides'.

As if that weren't enough, it was then possible to order from the newspaper's HQ a special giant-size 'My Club' card to take pride of place in the middle of the poster.

The Reds 'My Club' card is one of the rarest around.

To be frank, few punters made it this far down the line – making the Reds 'My Club' card (not to mention that of some of the smaller Third and Fourth Division teams) one of the rarest around. Especially in mint condition, as those that were ordered were almost inevitably slapped straight on to Junior's wall!

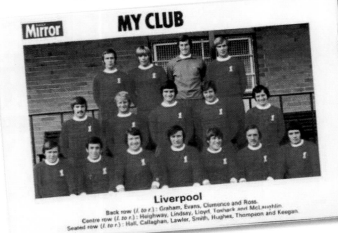

Liverpool
Back row (l. to r.): Graham, Evans, Clemence and Ross.
Centre row (l. to r.): Heighway, Lindsay, Lloyd, Toshack and McLaughlin.
Seated row (l. to r.): Hall, Callaghan, Lawler, Smith, Hughes, Thompson and Keegan.

The *Father Ted* perspective challenge: the small card is big and the big card is for away.

11

STAR SOC

SERIES OF

Buy the [

regularly to

your series

38

MIRRORCARD

RPOOL

SIDES

r

plete

Back row (*l. to r.*): Graham, Evans, Clemence and Ross.
Centre row (*l. to r.*) : Heighway, Lindsay, Lloyd, Toshack and McLaughlin.
Seated row (*l. to r.*): Hall, Callaghan, Lawler, Smith, Hughes, Thompson and Keegan.

The Anfield Experience: Guy Keeley's photos of
Liverpool v Bristol City, October 1979.

Blurred, big heads; action and fences trapped
like flies in aspic; bags of atmosphere, and 1-0
to the goodies.

DEBUT DAY
KK runs out of the Anfield tunnel for his debut against Forest on 14 August, 1971. He was on the scoresheet within 12 minutes as the Reds strolled the match 3-1, and went on to be the club's top scorer with 11.

The Name's Kevin. Kevin Keegan.

PANINI

Panini's first set of domestic League cards came out under the Top Sellers name in the '72, but it wasn't until later in the '70s that they hit their stride, producing uniform, trusted sticker sets which were actually sticky.

Under this onslaught, A&BC lost their way and were bought out by the American firm Topps, who temporarily brought a little baseball card razamatazz and glam-rock style to proceedings. Still, the days of cardboard were numbered - as were those of good old FKS, who responded to the Panini steamroller with their own sticky set of bizarre gold stickers in 1978 before quietly biting the dust.

The Panini revolution stood for reliability, professionalism, mass popularity and a return to hundreds

of near-identical head shots, albeit with little flags and team crests.

It seemed that everyone had a copy of that debut *Football 78* album in their school bag, along with a pile of swaps held in place with a laggy band. Our new favourite thing was twice as hefty as its predecessor, weighing in at a fat 64 pages; each club spread over two pages instead of one, and in total there were 525 stickers to collect.

The stickers themselves were beautifully designed, clear head-and-shoulders shots with a club badge and a St George's or St Andrew's flag because, yes, the Scots had been included too. Clydebank's Billy McColl got to have his own sticker, and the English Second Division was also covered with a team group and badge for each previously ignored team.

Ah, those badges. There was a heartbeat jump when you ripped open your packet and saw a gold foil Liverpool badge nestling among the half-dozen stickers...

Panini reigned for a good fifteen years, never straying far from their '78

RONNY ROSENTHAL
LIVERPOOL

The Three Ronnies: Here's Rosenthal, Yeast and Moran out of shot...

GARY GILLESPIE
LIVERPOOL

Defender. Born Stirling 5.7.60. Scottish international who started his career with Falkirk before moving to Coventry. Won 10 Under-21 caps prior to Liverpool signing him for £325,000 in 1983. Reliable, difficult to beat and covers the penalty area well.

GLENN HYSEN
LIVERPOOL

Defender. Born Gothenburg, Sweden 30.10.59. Swedish star international and captain who signed from Fiorentina of Italy for £600,000 in 1989. A sound tactician with good distribution, he is strong in the air, tackles solidly and has acute positional sense.

ALAN HANSEN
LIVERPOOL

Defender. Born Alloa 13.6.55. Versatile athlete who has represented Scotland Under-18s at golf, volleyball and squash. A classy and composed centre-back who has won 20 Scottish caps, he is a magnificent and influential leader who combines brilliance with reliability.

STEVE NICOL
LIVERPOOL

Born here 11.12.61. Liverpool's 'Mr Versatile' who has played with distinction in every back four position and in midfield since moving from Ayr United for £300,000 in 1981. Experienced Scottish international who is a highly skilled, determined and brave.

That between 1978 and 1981 Liverpool established a record run for a Football League club of 85 unbeaten Division 1 home games. They won 49 and drew the other 16, scoring 212 goals and conceding only 36. That when Liverpool played their first-ever League game in 1893, goalkeeper Bill McOwen was the only English player in the team. The other 10 were Scots.

JOHN BARNES
LIVERPOOL

PETER BEARDSLEY
LIVERPOOL

IAN RUSH
LIVERPOOL

FOOTBALL LEAGUE
FIRST DIVISION

Liverpool

Chairman: J.W. Smith JP
Manager: Bob Paisley
Secretary: Peter Robinson
Coach: Ron Moran
Captain: Emlyn Hughes
Year formed: 1892
Ground capacity: 56,318
Record attendance: 61,905 v Wolves, FA
Honours: Division One Champions: 1900-
1922-23, 1946-47, 1963-64, 1964-
1976-77 (These ten victories co
Division Two Champions: 1893-
1961-62.
FA Cup winners: 1965, 1974.
European Cup winners: 1977.
Colours: All red with white trim.
Change colours: White shirts with red
white stockings.

BOB PAISLEY (Manager)

RAY CLEMEN

blueprint, producing a series of highly collectable and well-loved albums until they, in turn, were replaced by Merlin around the time the Premier League was launched and the licensing fees leapt up.

The Panini *Football 1991* sticker album proudly bore the crests of the Football League and the PFA together with that of the Scottish League and pro body counterparts. What Panini didn't know was that Merlin (AKA good old Topps, if you read the small print) were waiting in the wings to scupper the comfy status quo with a deal already tied up with the brand-new Premier League.

In 1992, Panini's remaining PFA licence allowed them only to produce stickers of the players rather than any club details. How sad it was to see official stats replaced by weedy 'captain's comments' and it got worse when kits were no longer able to be shown – players trotted out in standard white PFA boiler suits – or else players' kit was recoloured in

lairy greens, reds and oranges in the utterly emasculated 'Super Players From Top Teams' of '96.

While Panini responded by skittering down the leagues for material, Merlin's *Premier League 1994* debut featured PL badges, team groups, full info and players in kits, bright and beautiful. There was even a page for Sky TV cards.

IAN RUSH

RONNIE WHELAN

LIVERPOOL

LIVERPOOL

LIVERPOOL

Anfield Stadium

LIVERPOOL

BRUCE GROBBELAAR
LIVERPOOL

BRUCE GROBBELAAR Goalkeeper. Born Zimbabwe. Ht. 6.0. Wt. 12.0. Age 26. Has been an ever present for two years in the Liverpool goal since taking over from Ray Clemence, completing 84 League appearances. Bought from Vancouver Whitecaps in March 1981 for £250,000 he had made his Football League debut originally with Crewe Alexandra against Wigan in December 1979. An international for Zimbabwe he has a spectacular style between the posts.

ALAN HANSEN Defender. Born Alloa. Ht. 6.1. Wt. 13.0. Age 26. Took his total of League appearances for the club to 195 at the end of 1982-83 having started his career with Partick Thistle where he had made 86 in the Scottish League. Plays in the middle of the back four and has won Under-21, Under-23 and full honours for Scotland. Signed by the Merseyside club in May 1977 for £100,000 and made his debut against Derby County in September that year. ■ 21 □ 0 (6).

ALAN HANSEN
LIVERPOOL

ALAN KENNEDY
LIVERPOOL

MARK LAWRENSON Defender. Born Preston. Ht. 5.11. Wt. 11.8. Age 26. Another utility player who can play equally well in midfield or as a defender. Was with Preston at first and made his League debut against Watford in April 1975. Moved to Brighton in July 1977 and to Liverpool in a £900,000 deal in August 1981. An experienced Republic of Ireland international he has also made a career total of 304 League appearances. 1982-83. ■ 21 □ 1 (6).

PHIL NEAL
LIVERPOOL

LIVERPOOL

PHIL NEAL

LIVERPOOL F.C.
Division One 1968-69

EMLYN HUGHES Liverpool

STEVE HEIGHWAY
Liverpool

THE BEDROOM SHRINE

You can rebuild it, y'know – the bedroom shrine of your youth when you loved them all, even the dodgy old full-back on whom the adults would pour scorn and derision.

When you wanted to see their images last thing at night and first thing in the morning; arranged in teamgroup ranks, watching over you while you slept.

The thrill of opening a *Goal*, or *Shoot!* or *Tiger* and seeing a real actual Liverpool hero featured on a colour poster – or, even better, a team photo in the centre spread – might not be so keen

now. But don't let that hold you back.

You can still get the horrible woodchip wallpaper we all had in our bedrooms, and paint it that turquoise light blue that was in vogue in the mid-Seventies. Someone will still have the recipe.

And there are people on eBay who make it their business to go through old magazines and annuals pulling out the Liverpool posters, flogging them by the dozen. The collection that took you seven years to accrue can now be obtained in a couple of days.

It won't have organically spread across your wall over the years like a fungus of devotion, but it will still look magnificent.

Almost certainly, the wife will understand.

PETER CORMACK
Liverpool and
Scotland

PETER THOMPSON
(Liverpool)

LIVERPOOL

BACK ROW: Geoff Strong, Gerry Byrne, Chris Lawler, Tommy Lawrence, Ray Clemence, Larry Lloyd, Ian Ross, Alec Lindsay.
FRONT ROW: Ian Callaghan, Alun Evans, Roger Hunt, Tommy Smith, Ron Yeats, Emlyn Hughes, Ian St. John, Peter Thompson, Bobby Graham.

TEAM SET | LIVERPOOL

BRIAN HALL   IAN CALLAGHAN   STEVE HEIGHWAY

...RBY...ND   ...Y CLEMENCE   TOMMY SMITH

...LLECT THE WHOLE SERIES!

...NDSAY Liverpool

L.F.C.
58

RAY KENNEDY
Liverpool

SHOOT

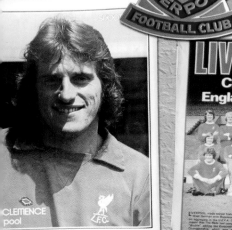

CLEMENCE
...pool

L.F.C.

LIVERPOOL~
Champions of
England and Europe

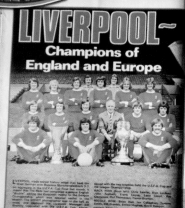

LIVERPOOL made soccer history when they beat the
...iliver German with Borussia Mönchengladbach 3-2
on aggregate in the U.E.F.A. Cup Final last month. It
meant that The Reds had completed a glorious English
"double" adding the European trophy to the League
Championship, which was secured earlier in the
season. The SHOOT photographer was on the spot to
snap captured here with the two trophies (left) the U.E.F.A. Cup and
(right) the League Championship.
BACK ROW (from left): Chris Lawler, Alec Lindsay,
John Toshack, Frank Lane, Larry Lloyd, Ray
Clemence, Phil Thompson, Trevor Storton.
MIDDLE ROW: Brian Hall, Ian Callaghan, Tommy
Smith, Bill Shankly, Peter Hughes, Kevin Keegan...

THE AUTOGRAPH BOOK

Gone out of existence. Withdrawn from the field. Abandoned. Missed. Passed by.

Everything we come across on this journey through the Lost World of Liverpool FC is no more. They thought it was all over – and they were dead right.

The autograph book was unlike any other of its day. Its cartridge-paper pages were blank, devoid of words and lines, with the built-in compensation of alternate pastel shades – chalky blue, green, pink, yellow. The outer corners of the pages were missing, rounded off so as not to offend the hand of an honoured victim. The spine of the leather-bound booklet ran down the short side, so it lolled open invitingly. On the cover of the book there was no author's name or title, just a single, golden word in a curly typeface. And then there was the vital loop of elastic to hold the book closed in the owner's back pocket, either encircling the whole precious volume, or just stretching over a single corner.

Lost. Let slip. No longer in our possession.

It isn't just the autograph book that has bitten the dust in recent years, but also the crowd of small boys hanging around the locked double doors marked PLAYERS AND OFFICIALS

ONLY an hour after the match. The players are missing, too: men who didn't need a minder at their side to talk to a twelve-year-old about the afternoon's brawls and cannonballs. Strong. Lawrence. Hughes. St John. The kind of players whose personally signed message you'd want to treasure forever.

The warning signs came when first two, then three, and now four of the five attackers in every team were phased out, goalscoring deemed surplus to requirement. Local heroes fell out of fashion. Red-faced stoppers failed to evolve with changing times, and so soon became extinct. And the best player in every team of the Sixties and Seventies became the first called up to the great kickaround in the sky.

All gone, but not forgotten.

Then as now, football magazines and club shops churned out sheets of pre-printed (quite literally auto-) autographs to help save the all-important stars time and hassle. It's all a question of supply and demand, see? But it's odd how much more charming the old sheets seem in comparison to today's handily pre-signed official postcards.

Strong. Lawrence. Hughes. St John.
The kind of players whose message
you'd want to treasure forever.

SUBBUTEO

Subbuteo was by far the most popular table-top representation of football, and its '00'-scale figures still hold a special place in the hearts of blokes across the globe. Part of the game's appeal was due to the huge range of accessories which, while unnecessary for the actual playing of the game, did prop up an illusion of realism and 'add to the big-match atmosphere'.

Plastic pitches were one of the ugliest developments in Eighties football. QPR, Luton and Oldham became unbeatable at home because they mastered the art of playing on a surface that had all the properties of lino – sliding tackles were out, except for players wearing motorcycle leathers under their shorts. Meanwhile, good old Subbuteo exhibited their usual dogged determination to keep up with the times, producing their own 'Astroturf' pitch – although, if their 'grass' pitch was made of green baize cloth, and the 'Astroturf' surface from slightly different baize cloth, it's unclear in what sense it was any more 'artificial'.

The rampant hooliganism of the time puts into stark perspective any complaints about plastic pitches, leading as it did to football attendances going down and spike-topped fences going up. Subbuteo didn't shirk its remit to mirroring the game and replaced its friendly green picket fences with prison railings and mounted police to keep any potential plastic yobboes off the pitch.

The actual Subbuteo playing figures of the late-Sixties to late-Seventies are known these days as Heavyweights, with their National Service haircuts, and a stance that suggested they were well up for it.

The Seventies also saw short-lived and unloved 'Scarecrows' and 'Zombies' figures, before the Eighties brought the more detailed, and more popular, 'Lightweights' which saw the Reds through the Crown Paints era.

Although accessories such as the dugouts and the ambulance men, the TV tower with mini-Motty, the floodlights and VIP figures (including Queenie handing over a tiny FA Cup) were affordable and always welcome on a Christmas morning, the ultimate prize had to be the Subbuteo stadium, complete with a decent crowd of ready-painted spectators. Unfortunately, they were beyond the pocket of most kids' parents and you'd count yourself lucky to have a single, foot-long stand with a couple of dozen spectators dotted around it.

The 'Heavyweight' figures of the Seventies had a stance that suggested they were **well up for it.**

4   5   6

We used to buy packs of unpainted spectators – fifty per box, all as naked as the day they were moulded – and only after weeks of eye-damaging work on Polo-Neck Man, Fatty, Celebrating Man and his equally Celebrating Girlfriend, did we discover the ultimate irony: with stands on all four sides it was virtually impossible to play the game without nudging a stand and causing a mini-stadium disaster.

Oh, come on, let's go up the park and play football.

59

BAB

The BAB Souvenir Company was known for just two, instantly recognisable products:

1 – The lairy, you might say imaginatively, coloured football club crest sticker

2 – The star-player sticker, always carefully labelled in case of any doubt as to who was depicted.

The modern-day attraction to collectors is essentially down to the fact that, in the early Seventies, hundreds of thousands of children simply couldn't resist unpeeling the backs of the stickers and attaching them to their school bags, school desks, bedroom walls and younger siblings, testing to the limit the proud boast on the retail cards:

"GREAT! Collect ALL these football 'club' badges," shouted the old counter box. "Sticks to almost any surface."

GREAT! Collect **ALL** these football 'club' badges.
Sticks to almost any surface.

It could almost have been a long-term strategy to boost values to collectors.

And then there's the sloppy way the company continually recycled their few sticker designs in new and unlikely colours, with endless minor variations, which appeals to the obsessive modern collector.

Admittedly, we mainly like them because they're funny. Is that the least flattering image of Alun Evans and Ian St John you ever did see? Ray Clemence is doing his best to stifle a snigger... but then he's no felt-pen painting himself!

TEAMS THAT YOU CAN RECITE

When teams were teams rather than private contractors of fleeting acquaintance, the first-choice line-up would go unchanged for seasons on end, with the boss blooding a kid or adding perhaps one new face over the close season, but only to replace the arthritic right-back who had just enjoyed his testimonial year.

You knew your team was a team because they piled into a team bath after the match, rather than wearing flip-flops and initialled dressing-gowns and insisting on private shower cubicles. You knew they were a team because their surnames seemed to rhyme when you recited them.

Clemence, Lawler, Lindsay, Smith, Lloyd, Hughes, Keegan, Cormack, Toshack, Heighway, Callaghan. What's the first Liverpool team you can automatically recite?

What's your first Liverpool side?

The one you can automatically recite...

Every year, you'd hear a news story about a fan who had named their firstborn after their whole beloved team. Take a bow, Raymond Christopher Alexander Thomas Laurence Emlyn Joseph Peter John Stephen Ian Blenkinsop. You'll be coming up 42, next birthday. And, of course, it's now a family tradition to name a little one after your heroes, even though it doesn't really work so well in the era of 40-strong Premier League squads.

So spare a thought for poor little Bradley Glen José Kolo Daniel Luis Luis Steven Iago Philippe Oussama Jordan Daniel Sebastián Mamadou Lucas Simon Joe Pepe Tiago Fabio Suso Raheem Jordon Martin Conor Samed Martin Jon Ryan Brad Jordan Andre Jerome Jack Cameron Lloyd Danny João Blenkinsop.

'Bra' for short. Smashing little girl.

TEAMS AND HALF-TI

LIVERPOOL
(Red Shirts)

1 Ray CLEMENCE
2 Chris LAWLER
3 Alec LINDSAY
4 Tommy SMITH (Capt.)
5 Larry LLOYD
6 Emlyn HUGHES
7 Kevin KEEGAN
8 Peter THOMPSON
9 Steve HEIGHWAY
10 John TOSHACK
11 Ian CALLAGHAN

Substitute:

Referee:
H. Williams
(Sheffield)

JACK SHARP
SPORT
LIVERPO

Linesman:
A. Parkinson
(Orange Flag)

LIVERPOOL

(Red Shirts)

1 Bruce GROBBELA.
2 Phil NEAL
3 Alan KENNEDY
4 Phil THOMPSON
5 Alan HANSEN
6 Mark LAWRENSON
7 Kenny DALGLISH
8 Ronnie WHELAN
9 Ian RUSH
10 Terry McDERMOTT
11 Graeme SOUNESS (Capt)

Substitute:

LIVERPOOL (Red-and-	
1	BRUCE GROBBEL/
2	GARY GILLESPIE
3	MARK LAWRENSO
4	STEVE NICOL
5	RONNIE WHELAN
6	ALAN HANSEN (Ca
7	PETER BEARDSLEY
8	JOHN ALDRIDGE
9	RAY HOUGHTON
10	JOHN BARNES
11	STEVE McMAHON
Subs	

6 Mic
7 Ian
8 Gly
9 Tre
10 Ra
11 Ste

Subst

RADIO

David 'Supersub' Fairclough
92 starts. 61 sub appearances. 55 goals.
Good lad!

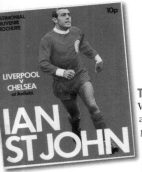

THE TESTIMONIAL MATCH

When was the last time you went along to pay your respects to a great old servant of your club, putting up with the prospect of a meaningless friendly against big local rivals – it's never quite the same, on their days off – in order to chip in to the loyal clubman's retirement nest egg as he looked forward to living in temporarily reduced circumstances and having to get a proper job? Eh?

There's no such thing as a testimonial match any more. Lining the pockets of a multi-millionaire with the proceeds of a kickaround against a team with the suffix 'XI' doesn't count. The vital elements of long service, need, mutual gratitude and respect are all absent.

Long service, need, mutual gratitude and respect.

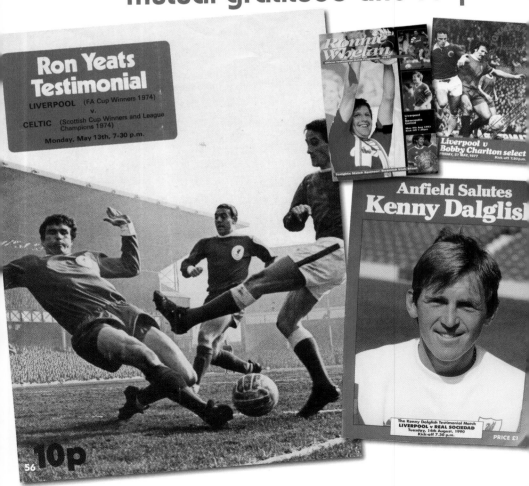

Liverpool

Ray Clemence

International Appearances	
International Goals	
League Appearances	
League Goals	
Height	

Liverpool

Steve Heighway

International Appearances	18
International Goals	1
League Appearances	269
League Goals	44
Height	5'10½"

Liverpool

Ray Kennedy

International Appearances	10
International Goals	2
League Appearances	266
Leag...	74
	5'11"

Liverpool

Phil Neal

International Appearances	9
International Goals	0
League Appearances	308
League Goals	44
Height	5'11"

TOP TRUMPS

Kids used to flip their cards at playground walls, either trying to get closest to the bricks or cover the oppo, and of course we jammed millions of pounds' worth of cards into the spokes of our bikes to get a groovily authentic engine noise.

Hence, Top Trumps were invented in the '70s to give card-owning a little more of a competitive dynamic:

Phil Neal… challenge me on League Appearances and you're going down in flames. International Goals, and he's all yours.

Then Ray Kennedy wipes the floor with poor old Ray Clemence in the League Goals stakes… but the long-serving goalie, it must be said, had a distinct half-inch advantage where it really mattered.

This head-to-head game-playing tradition was revived in the mid-'90s by Subbuteo Squads sets, and powers into the future with Shootout cards. But neither of them contain the word 'trump'.

How many pub-bound Reds fans could name Ray Kennedy's next two League sides? Swansea City and Hartlepool.

WE ALL SCREAM FOR ICE CREAM

We're guessing the ice cream industry hasn't had a great time of it recently, given the drizzly nature of our rather rubbish summers (notlikewhenwewerekids). Well, maybe they should start giving football badges away with their ice cream, like they did in 1971. That would soon

"Y'know when the chimes are going?

That means they've run out of ice-cream."

have us running to the end of the street every time we heard the chimes playing 'The Whistler and his Dog'.

Mister Softee issued their '1st Division Football League Club Badges' for the 1971-72 season, featuring the 22 top-flight clubs plus England and Wales... but not Scotland where, presumably, it's a bit chilly for ice-cream and lollies.

Rarer editions of this set, which was issued for one more season, were branded 'Lord Neilson' and 'Tonibell'.

Was it just our dads that said: "You know when the chimes are going? That means they've run out of ice cream"?

PAYING AT THE GATE

It's frowned upon, these days, is cash. You can't just walk up to a football ground clutching a wad of used tenners and expect to pay their exorbitant admission fee. You could be anyone, see? You might get to go in the wrong end, and there'd be hell to pay as well as 50 quid. You might be a troublemaker. You might be a terrorist or a money launderer. Cash is an evil temptation, just one short step from potential corruption. The chairman has warned us there's a lot of it going on.

You can't just pay to get in. Oh, no. You have to be a club member, and to facilitate membership we'll need to see your passport, driving licence and a matching utility bill for an address within the county. You need a ticket with a computer key code to gain access to the stadium. And tickets can only be purchased in advance, subject to a two pound booking fee.

Back in the day, all you had to do was turn up at the turnstiles.

Send money in advance, and the secretary of Liverpool FC would promptly send it back with a kind but forceful typewritten note. Just turn up on the day, good sir. Be sure and come early! And a splendid time is guaranteed for all...

If you enclosed a remittance it is returned herewith to you.

Liverpool Football Club
and Athletic Grounds Co. Ltd.

Manager : W. Shankly
Secretary : P. B. Robinson
Telephone : ANField 2361/2

ANFIELD ROA
LIVERPOOL -

Date as Postmark

Dear Sir or Madam,

Season 1968/69.

With reference to your recent enquiry, we have to inform you that all Stand Tickets for League Matches at Anfield this season have been fully sold.

For your information admission to the paddock and ground at these matches will, unless otherwise announced in the press, be by payment at the turnstiles.

If you enclosed a remittance it is returned herewith to you. Postal Orders cross and made payable to the Club, can, providing the counterfoil is also produced, be cashed by you at the Post Office.

Yours faithfully,
P B Robinson
Secretary.

Birthplace Liverpool: Aha, so this must be a magazine page from the olden days...

FOCUS ON...

Back in 1973, Brian William Hall of Glasgow lay to shame every modern footballer who ever filled in a programme questionnaire name-dropping property portfolios and £750 cocktails.

He didn't like liver or kidneys; travelling was just the biggest drag in soccer; and failing that exam at Uni was a big disappointment.

But put some Pentangle on his hi-fi, or sit him down in front of Morecambe & Wise with a Chinese, and you'd have a very contented man. Especially if you invited an astronaut round into the bargain.

And big Raymond Clemence from Skegness tells it like it is. Or rather was.

CAR: Lancia Beta.
FAVOURITE OTHER TEAM: Leeds United.
BEST COUNTRY VISITED: West Germany.
FAVOURITE FOOD: Any fish.
FAVOURITE SINGERS: Carpenters, Andy Williams, Diana Ross.

Ray hated being pestered when he was out for a meal with his wife, unless, presumably, it was by Barbra Streisand or Muhammad Ali.

We wish Ray the best of luck with his PROFESSIONAL AMBITION: To play in the 1978 World Cup Finals....

Perhaps if he'd been born in Loch Ness rather than Skegness?

Chicken in a basket, gym teacher, Raquel Welch and Benny Hill.

FOCUS ON
RAY CLEMENCE
Liverpool

NAME: Raymond Clemence
PLACE: Skegness
ATE: 5th August, 1948
TE: 12st 7lb.
CUS CLUB: Scunthorpe United
ED: Yes
REN: Two daughters
ancia Beta
OURITE PLAYER: Ian Callaghan
OURITE OTHER TEAM: Leeds United
er of Leicester City
ST DIFFICULT OPPONENT: Keith
T MEMORABLE MATCH: Beating
castle in the 1974 F.A. Cup Final
T THRILL: Winning my first
and cap
ST DISAPPOINTMENT: Losing the
pionship by one point in 1972
COUNTRY VISITED: West

Germany
FAVOURITE FOOD: Any fis
MISCELLANEOUS LIKES: f
at home with my family
MISCELLANEOUS DISLIK
pestered when out for a m
vels; people who are alwa
appointments
FAVOURITE T.V. SHOWS:
documentaries
FAVOURITE SINGERS: Ca
Williams, Diana Ross
FAVOURITE ACTOR/ACT
Newman, Barbra Streisand
BEST FRIEND: Team-mat
BIGGEST INFLUENCE ON
late Alan Bushby, coach at
BIGGEST DRAG IN SOCC
back after an away defeat

FOCUS ON
BRIAN HALL
Liverpool

FULL NAME: Brian William Hall
BIRTHPLACE: Glasgow
BIRTHDATE: November 22nd, 1946
HEIGHT: 5ft. 5in.
WEIGHT: 9st. 7lb.
PREVIOUS CLUBS: None
MARRIED: Yes
CAR: Cortina
FAVOURITE PLAYER: George Best
FAVOURITE OTHER TEAM: Preston
MOST DIFFICULT OPPONENT: Everton (all
eleven of them)

MOST MEMORABLE MATCHES: The 1971
F.A. Cup Semi-Final against Everton and the
Final against Arsenal
BIGGEST THRILL: Scoring the winner in the
above Semi-Final
BIGGEST DISAPPOINTMENT: Failing an
exam at University
BEST COUNTRY VISITED: Sardinia (Italy)
FAVOURITE FOOD: Chinese
MISCELLANEOUS LIKES: Cars, hi-fi, my
home
MISCELLANEOUS DISLIKES: Liver, kidneys,
carrots
FAVOURITE T.V. SHOWS: Documentaries,
Morecambe & Wise

FAVOURITE SINGERS: The Beatles, The
Nice, Pentangle
FAVOURITE ACTORS: Peter O'Toole, Paul
Newman, Richard Burton
BEST FRIEND: My wife
BIGGEST INFLUENCE ON CAREER: My
Manager Bill Shankly
INTERNATIONAL HONOURS: None
BIGGEST DRAG IN SOCCER: Travelling
PERSONAL AMBITION: To do well in every
game I play
PROFESSIONAL AMBITION: As above
IF YOU WEREN'T A FOOTBALLER WHAT
DO YOU THINK YOU'D BE? A teacher
WHAT PERSON IN THE WORLD WOULD
YOU MOST LIKE TO MEET? An astronaut

Scouser James Robert Case is going Dutch with his **FAVOURITE OTHER SIDE:** Holland's national team, **FAVOURITE PLAYER:** Johan Cruyff, and **BEST COUNTRY VISITED:** Holland.

While Bangor's own Joey Jones (who if he hadn't become a footballer would be 'A nobody') dispels the myth that his **FAVOURITE FOOD** is frogs' legs.

It is, in fact...
Mashed potatoes.

MARSHALL CAVENDISH FOOTBALL HANDBOOK

Long before the age of YouTube or even the ubiquitous video recorder, there was no easy way to replay golden goals from the past – you just had to wait for them to be reshown on *Football Focus*, which could often prove quite a lengthy wait if you were waiting for a specific goal.

For most fans, there was some respite available thanks to the *Marshall Cavendish Football Handbook* ("in 873 weekly parts") and their smashing arrow- and dot-laden diagrams which traced the build-up to a goal in stunning time-lapse ImaginationVision – complete with added slight confusion!

It's just like being there in 1977 as Terry McDermott cracks in the Reds' opener against Borussia Moenchengladrags.

The Heighway twins outwit a nameless German out on the right wing before slipping in a through-ball that leaves two more white-clad spectators gasping for breath. And so it falls to the Terry Mac twins to crack in the first goal in the 3-1 European Cup triumph – and the German goalie doesn't even move from the canny position he's assumed lying in the goal area. You just had to be there...

The Marshall Cavendish arrow-and-dot diagram shows every
goal in stunning ImaginationVision,
complete with added slight confusion!

IMPROVE YOUR FOOTBALL   Action replay...   Action replay...   Action replay...   Action replay...   Action replay

McDermott's master move

The goal Terry McDermott scored against Borussia was a real Liverpool goal. It wasn't just about fitness and skill . . . it was also full of enthusiasm for the game.' GRAHAM TAYLOR

The stunning goal that put Liverpool on the road to their first European Cup triumph showed in a few marvellous seconds what that club is all about.

A typically sharp Liverpool build-up down the right led to a delightful through pass by Steve Heighway to Terry McDermott, who had made an amazing 60-yard run from his own half of the pitch into the Borussia penalty area.

McDermott's finishing matched the rest of the move, a sweet shot across the Borussia keeper and into the corner of the net.

Callaghan, as ever, started the move after winning the ball by the half-way line. He played a quick pass to Heighway and followed up to support him on the outside. This gave Heighway what every player needs: alternatives. He took the ball inside, and as two Borussia defenders came at him he played one of the most devastating balls in football—the one between two defenders which puts them out of the game.

So it had just about everything: Callaghan's tigerish tackle to win the ball in the first place, followed by his unselfish run.

Heighway showed skill and confidence to bring the ball inside and then needed to play the ball at the perfect weight for McDermott's run.

And what a run! It demanded a level of awareness for which Liverpool, with their great traditions of strength and character, are not given enough credit.

Looking back, this goal was the one that helped to establish McDermott as a goalscoring midfield player.

He followed up with a hat-trick against Kevin Keegan's SV Hamburg in the second leg of the Europe Super Cup at Anfield.

Graham Taylor's analysis
'Liverpool at their best—when you've got players as honest as that, your problems are few. By honest, I mean players who make the kind of runs that Callaghan and McDermott put in to make that move possible—not only once, either, but whenever it's needed in a match. I'll tell you one thing—if McDermott had shot wide, he would have made the same run three minutes later !

'And don't just put it down to the standard of fitness that Liverpool demand. There's another quality that doesn't get enough attention . . . real enthusiasm. They made those runs because they've got it—they love the game and they want the ball, a very basic requirement but one that keeps Callaghan running about like a teenager. If you're finished when you stop enjoying the game, Callaghan will carry on for ever. He's a great example to every youngster.

Left captions on diagram:
HEIGHWAY 1
CALLAGHAN
HEIGHWAY 2
McDERMOTT 1
McDERMOTT 2

Heighway's through pass puts two defenders out of the game and McDermott has time to check on the keeper's position after his 60-yard run . . .

**In weekly parts
30p**

THE MARSHALL CAVENDISH

PART 7

FOOTBALL HANDBOOK

Y McDERMOTT
KROL
N HODDLE
JOHNSTONE
N PETERS

● **THE STARS IN ACTION**   ● **FACTS & FEATURES**

**In weekly parts
30p**

THE MARSHALL CAVENDISH

FOOTBALL HANDBOO

**IMPROVE YOUR SKILL AND INCREASE YOUR KNOWLED
WITH THE PROFESSIONA**

KENNY'S FROM HEAVEN
PROFILE OF THE
KOP'S NEW IDOL

's apprentice

IAMS
AMPS

FOOTBALL HANDBOOK

FOOTBALL HANDBOOK

FOOTBALL HANDBOOK

FOOTBALL HANDBOOK

Kenny's From
Heaven: One of those
golden 'I'll get my coat'
sub-editor moments.

WEMBLEY

"Based on the English Football Association Challenge Cup Competition, the most gripping features and exciting uncertainties of which it reproduces with vivid and truly amazing fidelity…"

No one plays board games any more: it's all down to attention span and lack of imagination and wanting excitement served up on a plate instead of having to work at it. And that's just us, never mind the kids.

It was the thrill of the Cup draw and the possibility of an alternate-universe upset that used to make Wembley so addictive. The reproduction of all those associations and assumptions that electrify the simple twinning of two clubs' names ("And it's Liverpool… at home to… Leeds United"… or "Accrington Stanley"… or "Everton"… we could go on).

It was the tension inherent in the inevitable reduction of 32 clubs to an historic final pairing. The chance to witness a spunky lower-league outfit confound the Darwinian bias that enabled top clubs to make more money, to spend it on star players, to score more goals… and even claim the right to throw loaded dice.

"The earning ability of clubs varies greatly, as does their playing ability," stated the Rules of the Game.

"Good Luck ! May the dice roll well for you, and may your favourite team appear many times in the final of the Cup at WEMBLEY."

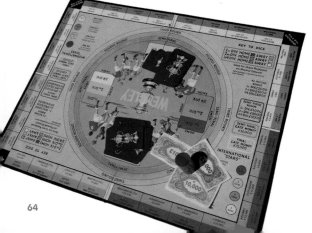

"Each club has a value (representing gate receipts) and each Division has different colour dice for Home and Away matches. These dice are specially produced to give a built-in advantage both to teams in higher divisions and to teams playing at Home."

The powerful red First Division Home die could roll 0, 1, 2, 3 or two chances of a 4, while the white Third/Fourth Division Away die was lumbered with two 0s and two 1s – plus a potentially giant-killing 4 and a 5 to spice things up.

Bring on Newtown! (History buffs, get Googling!)

GOALIES WITHOUT GLOVES

How we miss them, those Jolly Green Giants of our youth who only wore gloves when it was peeing down and there was a 'greasy surface'.

Only in retrospect does it become apparent how brave the gloveless goalies must have been. Every schoolboy in the country knew that Peter Lorimer could strike a ball at 70mph, and the likes of Ray Clemence had to willingly put their hands in the way.

A couple of years ago, I was playing five-a-side and took my turn in goal, bravely chucking the proffered gloves into the back of the net and springing into action.

Five hours later as I finally left casualty with my pinky bone back inside my skin, where it belongs, a lightbulb came on above my head: "Ahh... so *that's* why they wear gloves."

THE RATTLE

The other day, I wandered down to the football from the pub and took my seat at one minute to kick-off, as usual, in order to avoid any kind of 'match-experience' shenanigans. Before I could sit down I had to extricate an object from the laggy band that secured it to my seat.

It was a folded sheet of laminated card in

all but ruined the 2010 World Cup for me (along with England's risible performance), while some people thought they were such splendid fun, they started to take them to League

games the following season.

The football rattle enjoyed its heyday in the 1960s, when they became as iconic a symbol of football-supporterdom as the scarf and bobble-hat.

club colours, called a 'clap-banner', which explained the horrendous noise that had assaulted my eardrums since I'd entered the ground.

Needless to say, I immediately took against it.

But when the frenzied clacking had died down a bit, I did at least concede that my age was partly to blame. For I once received a football rattle for my birthday that made a quite spectacular noise when I whizzed it round my head. So much so, that its use had to be rationed in the house.

One (young) person's great sound is another (old) person's unholy racket. That explains why the vuvuzela

They were nearly always homemade, employing the sort of engineering skills that only Dad could manage, and painted up in glossy club colours with the team name added as a finishing touch.

What modern day Health & Safety laws would have to say about spinning a fairly hefty chunk of wood at speed round your head in a tightly packed crowd, I don't know.

"You'll have someone's eye out," probably.

One (young) person's great sound is another (old) person's unholy racket.

Beardo:

A bit of all right.

SHOOT!

SHOOT!

Allowed one comic a week, I'd already graduated from the entry-level *Beano* to *Scorcher*, but not until the summer of 1974, while immersed in the West Germany World Cup, did I consider myself man enough to step up to *Shoot!*

Eight pence was the price of admission, and I was soon in beyond the full-colour cover of Billy Bremner playing for Scotland against Brazil.

Now I could dive headlong into an article by Bobby Moore – every week, he'd let us backstage, behind the scenes in the life of a living, breathing football hero – and what's more I could puzzle over the fiendish problems posed in 'You Are the Ref'; study up-close World Cup action featuring Australia, Scotland, Holland, Zaire, DDR and Yugoslavia; chortle at the 'Football Funnies'; 'Focus On' Paul Gilchrist of Southampton (Miscellaneous Likes: motor racing, oil painting, music), and realise there were people just like me all over the country, courtesy of the 'Goal Lines' letters page and 'Ask the Expert' readers' queries.

If I was lucky, there'd be a full-page

star poster to add to my
shrine, though this only
happened once in a blue
moon. It's difficult to explain
now how a photo could be so
prized, Blu-Tacked instantly
up on your wall, but in the
days of black newsprint papers
and monochrome TV, the eight
colour pages in *Shoot!* were like
oases in a grey desert.

For five years my collection
grew, filling several boxes, until
1979 when my head was finally
turned by an attractive newcomer
called *Match Weekly*.

I'm sorry I dropped you, *Shoot!*,
and I'm even sorrier that we now
live in a world where kids can't leg
it down to the newsagents to eagerly
pore over the latest issue.

MOBIL BADGES

We love these silk badges given away with Mobil petrol in the early 80s.

When was the last time you visited a petrol station to be gifted a football collectable that you thought was worth holding on to for 30 years, fer chrissakes?

Made of pure 100% silk from a silkworm's bottom * and, as such, suitable for stitching on to your Sunday best anorak or parka?

Free with four gallons of 4-star.

The only downside, associated more with the free giveaway poster than the patches themselves, was the prospect of a giant Alan Hudson marauding down the country like King Kong or Godzilla or worse – Dribble of Destruction Horror Shock – stomping down his non-shooting boot worryingly close to the vicinity of our beloved capital city.

* Or possibly some kind of cheap polyester.

Remember Mobil? How about Texaco? Jet? Cleveland? Amoco? Chevron?

70

CASDON SOCCER

This system of pirouetting players, ball-bearing ball and wildly undulating pitch surface was a big seller over the years from the 1960s into the 80s, and Casdon's 'Item No. 150' went through several rebrands. After Bobby Charlton's retirement, King Kenny Dalglish put his name to the Soccer Game and even posed with Tom Cassidy, MD of the miniature marvel manufacturer – then in the 80s it became the England Squad Soccer Game with Paul Mariner, Kevin Keegan, Bryan Robson and Garry Birtles challenging the rules of perspective by crowding round the playing surface along with two small children on the box photo.

According to the online Casdon Toy Museum, "Some say it was probably the best football game of all time" – although that bumpy pitch and the crude one-colour players both intruded into the game's proudly touted 'realism'.

I'll admit that a pitch consisting of dramatic troughs and peaks wasn't something that taxed my imagination too much. Our school pitch was sited on a field that had been employed for strip farming during medieval times. Several centuries after the enclosure of England's land our field of

dreams still stubbornly consisted of ridges and furrows. A charge down the right wing was literally an up-and-down experience, and particularly small full-backs standing in particularly deep furrows could almost be hidden from view. A useful, if underhand, ambush tactic.

I don't think our Kenny would have endorsed that.

Casdon cogwheel close-up action: Come on, you Reds!

Champions!

Boxer John Conteh joins the lads of Liverpool to parade their trophies through the city in 1973.

TOPICAL TIMES

Strictly speaking, the *Topical Times* wasn't the most topical of newspapers in the Sixties and Seventies, having gone under in the Forties... but that didn't stop them producing annual football books right into the new millennium.

Always a welcome addition to a Christmas morning pillowcase, the presentation was lively in design, picture led, and featured a seemingly never-ending supply of different fonts.

Apart from the punchy tabloid-style headlines and clippy titbits, 'Their Other Team' was always a favourite staple spread, enabling us junior peeping Toms to keep tabs on what star players, their wives and kids were getting up to, relaxing at home in suburbia. Here were huge rounded collars; kids in polo necks; flock wallpaper that has allegedly come back into fashion; velour sofas in a greeny-browny-goldy colour that no longer exists; and the sort of brick feature fireplace you could only attempt if you had a few quid.

And, best of all, there were glossy colour pages that showed up every stitch of the old cotton shirts and ragged badges. And Liverpool on the cover, in the particularly Golden Years...

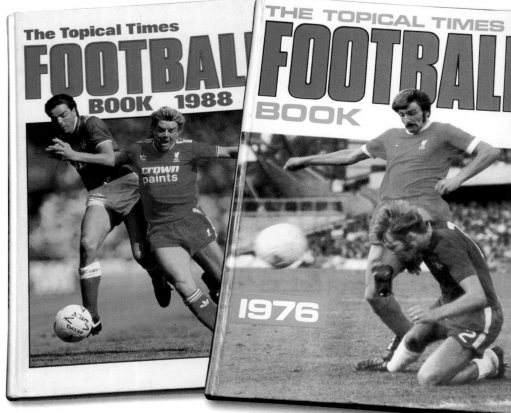

Topical: Well, it was at the time.

FA CUP CENTENARY COINS

Good old Esso. Every year, they brought out something great for us to collect, and 1972 was no different. The handsome 'FA Cup Centenary 1872-1972' brochure and coin collection was such a must-have item for every young boy that silence must surely have descended on the forecourts of Shell garages while the offer was on, with tumbleweed blowing around between deserted BP, Jet and Cleveland pumps.

There were 30 of these "silver-bright, superbly-minted Centenary Coins" to collect, one per visit to the Esso station, the album to house them in representing a modest Dad Tax of 15p.

Swap yer 29 coins – from the Wanderers and Blackburn Olympic to the big gold-coloured centrepiece coin minted later, a week after Leeds United's Wembley victory over Arsenal – all for the one Liverpool coin commemorating that proud Saturday afternoon back in 1965, the Reds' greatest FA Cup moment in history... to date.

Liverpool's greatest FA Cup moments in history... to date.

Esso extra: No matter how low the petrol gauge, it had to be an Esso station in the 70s.

POSING IN YOUR KIT

It was a magic feeling, pulling on your team's shirt, shorts and socks. And then looking down at the badge. It was the kind of occasion that warranted pestering your mother to get the camera out.

"Mam, take it now. Take it while I'm doing this..."

Waiting impatiently between shots while she 'wound it on'.

Standing up with your arms folded, with one foot on the ball, or crouched down holding the ball with splayed out fingers... it wasn't your mam anymore, it was the official club photographer on photocall day, taking the photo that would appear in *Shoot!* or on a football card. Or else you were your club's brand new signing, and a gaggle of snappers from the dailies were crowded round you.

"I think I've come to the end of the film," says Mam as her winder-onner meets resistance.

"Take it anyway!" you implore, arms spread out, for the perfect slow-motion volley.

The Liverpool Look for 1988: Kit, bobbles, scarf 'n' sticker style at the Charity Shield.

"Mam, quick, take it now.
Take it while I'm doing this..."

LIVERPOOL

SIMON
KIDD

SCOTTISH SUPERSTARS

Up until twenty years ago, every great First Division team in football history had included at least one Scot, usually the brains of the operation – the ball player, the stopper who could do more than just stop, or the unstoppable goalscorer. Mackay. Law. Bremner…

From the very top: the devastating Liverpool side of the Sixties was spearheaded by Ian St John, and the team of the Seventies and Eighties rocked on the fulcrum of Hansen, Souness and/or Dalglish.

The Reds' legendary boss Bill Shankly would never have got away with saying, "Although I'm a Scot, I'd be proud to be called a Scouser," if he hadn't been a Scot.

"It's fantastic," Shanks said about representing his country. "You look down at your dark blue shirt, and the wee lion looks up at you and says 'Get out after those English bastards!'"

Choose fitba.

Oor King Kenny, off to win the 1978 World Cup...

If there were a World Cup for value, Avenger would win it.

AVENGER

CHRYSLER
UNITED KINGDOM

The Chrysler Avenger.
Style, toughness. And a Championship performance.

ESPAÑA 82 — KENNY DALGLISH SCOTLAND

ESPAÑA 82 — GRAEME SOUNESS SCOTLAND

ESPAÑA 82 — ALAN HANSEN SCOTLAND

Wot, no Graeme Souness?
No Archie Gemmill?
No Joe Jordan?

LEARN THE GAME

It's over to Mr Logic of *Viz Comic* fame for your Anglo Confectionery top football tip of the day (well, actually, a day that's now somewhat buried in the relevance stakes, somewhere back in 1970).

It looks like the *Viz* lads also had a hand in drawing Trevor Brooking on the Ian Callaghan card, a random surly imposter on the Saint's big bubble-gum moment… and whatever happened to Roger Hunt?

"Corner kicks," Logic informs us, are "often a sound chance for scoring, having as their object delivering the ball to a player in the goal mouth who can divert it into the goal.

"Except, it must be clearly stated, in the case of a goal scored direct from the corner quadrant."

Tricked and Trapped
by a Tricky Trapper:
"Still" the ball with
Roger Hunt.

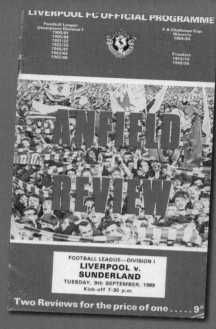

FULLY PROGRAMMED
Friday 1st January 1988 v Coventry City
The Kenny Dalglish Column
"In the ten years that I've been at Anfield, games against Coventry in the First Division have produced 32 goals to us and only two to the Sky Blues; and that's a record of which we can be proud..."

Sporting Heroes
Gary Gillespie chooses Ian Botham, Jack Nicklaus, Franz Beckenbauer... and his boss Kenny Dalglish.
You'll Never Walk Alone, if you become a member of the Liverpool FC Supporters' Club. Apply to The Secretary, 212 Lower Breck Road, Liverpool 6.

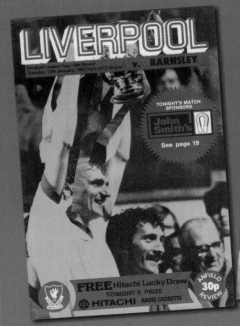

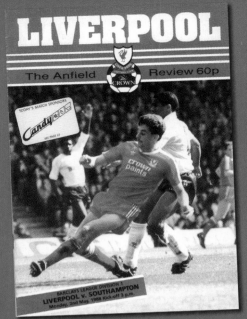

LIVERPOOL
The Anfield Review 60p

LIVERPOOL V. SOUTHAMPTON
Monday, 2nd May, 1988 Kick-off 3 p.m.

Season 1978-79
LEAGUE
DIVISION 1
Monday
1 January, 1979
Kick-off 3 p.m.

ANFIELD
REVIEW
20p

LIVERPOOL versus ASTON VILLA

Today's match sponsored by
ARROWSMITH
& LAKER
see inside page 18

The Years of Glory - 1972-73

"As it turned out Leicester didn't lose - but neither did Liverpool, so we were proclaimed champions in front of our ecstatic supporters. At the end Bill Shankly phoned home to tell his wife. "We've done it, Nessie... there's nae-one who can take it away from us now!"

Barclays League Division One
1. Liverpool - P 21 W 16 D 5 L 0 Pts 53
2. N Forest - P 20 W 13 D 4 L 3 Pts 43
3. Arsenal - P 22 W 12 D 4 L 6 Pts 40

If you are looking for a function room with a difference, Anfield is the place! Prestigious and excellently-appointed, the Executive Suite is ideal for lunches, dinners and wedding receptions...

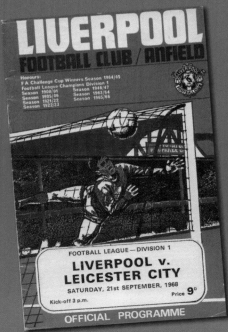

LIVERPOOL
FOOTBALL CLUB / ANFIELD

Honours:
F A Challenge Cup Winners Season 1964/65
Football League Champions Division 1
Season 1900/01   Season 1946/47
Season 1905/06   Season 1963/64
Season 1921/22   Season 1965/66
Season 1922/23

FOOTBALL LEAGUE — DIVISION 1
LIVERPOOL v. LEICESTER CITY
SATURDAY, 21st SEPTEMBER, 1968
Kick-off 3 p.m.   Price 9ᴰ

OFFICIAL PROGRAMME

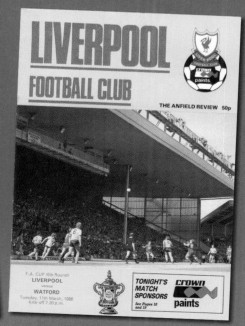

LIVERPOOL
FOOTBALL CLUB

THE ANFIELD REVIEW 50p

F.A. CUP (6th Round)
LIVERPOOL
versus
WATFORD
Tuesday, 11th March, 1986
Kick-off 7.30 p.m.

TONIGHT'S
MATCH
SPONSORS
See Pages 10 and 19

crown
paints

MILK

Whatever happened to milk? Milk used to be really important.

It was so important that you had to drink it at school, nicely warmed by the radiators in mini bottles, whether you wanted it or not. So important that it had to be delivered direct to your door, every day. Most mornings, I would be awoken by the whirring electric float, the clinking bottles and cheery off-key whistling of our milkman.

Of course, there were always strong links between milk and football.

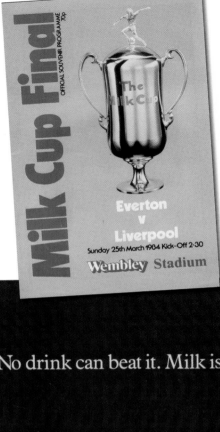

His name was Ernie: And he drove the fastest milk cart in the West.

No drink can beat it. Milk is

In the days of the terracing, what to do if you were a kid standing among adults, if you were a person of restricted growth, or even a bit of a shortarse? The solution for many was to obtain a milk crate that had gone astray from the local dairy, and to teeter on it for the duration of the game.

Use your milkman

The post-match FA Cup Final interviews always showed the victorious winners swigging milk by the gallon, filling the trophy with it and knocking that back, too.

Then, between 1982 and 1986, we literally had a Milk Cup when the Dairy Council sponsored the League Cup for four seasons. This led to the surreal sight of an eight-foot pint of milk occupying the centre-circle before every game.

The message was clear. If you wanted to be a footballer, you'd better start drinking as much milk as you can possibly get down yourself.

And then, somehow, milk fell out of favour. Suddenly it went from being essential to life, keeping your bones from crumbling and your teeth from falling out, to being bad for you in so many complicated ways.

No drink can beat it. Milk is supreme.

supreme

Phil Neal scores the winner, so he gets the best seat in the house. But they all get the best drink in the fridge. In fact, milk is so full of natural goodness, it's more than just a drink – it's liquid food. For sheer deliciousness and energy replacement, you can't beat the 'magic potion'.

By now John Barnes had volleyed a bottle of isotonic Lucozade into the changing room bin, and cow juice seemed to lose its appeal.

We don't have a milkman any more. We get our milk like you probably get yours, semi-skimmed in four-pint plastic containers from the supermarket. Just another thing on the shopping list.

I can't see anyone building a sex-romp film starring Robin Askwith around that premise.

MATCH WEEKLY

Match Weekly was launched on 6 September 1979, three weeks into the 1979-80 season, by Peterborough-based publishers EMAP. Editor Melvyn Bagnall declared: "Our object is simple... to improve on anything currently available." By which, of course, he

meant *Shoot!*, which had enjoyed a relatively unopposed decade of market dominance.

What immediately grabbed this 13-year-old about the newcomer on the newsagent's shelf was the way it was printed right to the edge, making *Shoot!*'s white borders suddenly look very passé.

Inside there was a stellar line-up of writers: Coppell, Atkinson, Keegan, Clough, Ardiles and Jimmy Hill. Instead of 'Focus On' there was 'Match Makers',

Pub Quiz:
Can your mate name Phil Neal's three Football League sides? Northampton (1pt), Liverpool (0pts!) and Bolton (1pt).

A stellar line-up of writers:

Kevin Keegan... plus Big Ron and Jimmy Hill.

with loads more questions. There were more colour pages, and 'Match Facts' with marks out of ten for every player in every game. And, just in case anyone was still dithering about parting with their 25p, there was a free Transimage sticker album thrown into the mix.

After a five-year love affair with *Shoot!*, I jumped ship to *Match* in an instant. And I wasn't the only one. After a long battle, *Match* eventually won out with a higher circulation.

THE KULT OF KEVIN KEEGAN

In the mid-70s, as in any decade of towering cultural significance, it was possible to gauge the social, psychological and sexual impact of any celebrity by the number of times they managed to take their top off in public, the number of unwarranted novelty hits they crammed under their belt, the number of toys and games using their name as a magnet to attract the schoolboy/girl dollar at Christmas time, the spiralling national sympathy rating following a heroic bike accident on *Superstars*, and the percentage of builders who miraculously started sprouting hairstyles in imitation of their hero.

Keggie the Kuddly Kutey
Was the ace face of Brut after-shave and Pirelli slippers

As the 70s tripped over their stack-heel soles into the barren Thatch-wracked 80s, Kevin Keegan – Ickle Keggie Keedle, everybody's favourite Kuddly Kutey – was no longer merely the ace face of Brut, the Green Cross Code and Pirelli slippers but also history's most-missed English exile plying his trade in Germany.

Cheers! "Hand on heart, you can't beat the great taste of Brut."

"**Don't cross near parked cars**" *says Kevin Keegan*

BE SMART BE SAFE

Use the Green Cross code

RKD 81 ON

PLAY BETTER SOCCER

with **KEVIN KEEGAN**

THE FAST BREAK...

Go forward Fifteen yards

KEVIN KEEGAN **MASTER CARD**

Use this card for any move you like:
• To SCORE if you are Ten yards from goal or nearer.
• To SAVE! or cancel out your opponent's goal.
• To SAVE! a penalty.
• As a twenty yard pass

...his card to ...ike!

Tackle!

This card cancels out your opponent's last move

My advice is, don't hold back or be faint-hearted when a tackle has to be made. The secret is, keep your weight over the ball, and your eye on it at all... One of the best I've se...

Check out the horrors of that elusive second hit on YouTube: "When the lonely nights / Are drawing in / I long to be with you / In England..." indeed.

...in love

KEVIN KEEGAN

KEVIN KEEGAN

THE IDOL OF ANFIELD

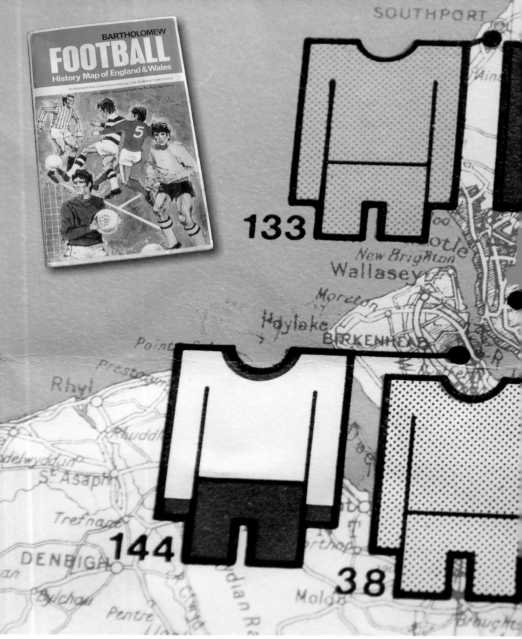

BARTHOLOMEW MAP

In the early 1970s John Bartholomew & Son produced the 'Football History Map of England and Wales' as part of their series of pictorial and historical maps... Created by John Carvosso, the stylised square kits and re-rendered club crests gave it an iconic look that remains hugely popular among football supporters. In the years just before more intricate kit designs arrived this was all that was required.

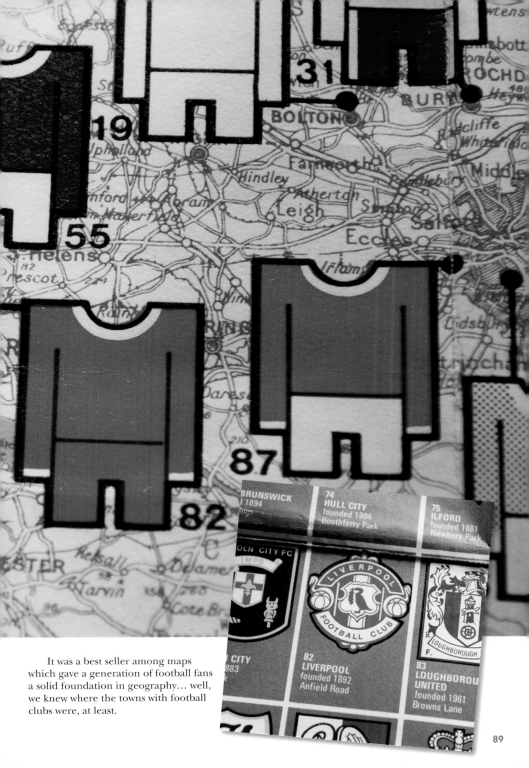

It was a best seller among maps which gave a generation of football fans a solid foundation in geography… well, we knew where the towns with football clubs were, at least.

| A580 | East Lanca... ... Motorway | ... | ... | 18 miles |

M6   South for 6... ... exit No...
M6 Service... ... ... miles

A5   West for 2... ... ...
     A449 ... ...

Wolverham... ... A449 approaching
the Town C... ... and Police
Parking in ...

MOTORING AWAY

The sheer naivety of the Liverpool FC furry dice, the Reds mini-kit, the red, yellow and white wooden-beaded car seat and the David Fairclough 'Soundly Grounded'-brand electro-static back-bumper earthing device is enough to whisk you back to a time when motoring away was a real expedition – an adventure and a treat on the A-roads of England when they were cluttered with Minis and Morris Minors and transport caffs. Steering sensibly in your string-sided driving gloves, you were guided by the *AA Book of the Road*, stewed cuppas on glass-top tables – and, eventually, the beckoning of floodlight pylons.

It's time to rediscover the joys of a tactical team-talk with salt and pepper pots in a giant puddle-strewn layby.

One of the most enjoyable elements of the away trip is the camaraderie shared with fellow supporters, so be sure to make yourself instantly identifiable as a motorised football fan. Car coats and bobble-hat combos are tops in this respect, with a silk or knitted scarf in club colours recommended to be trapped flapping from your rear windows or quarterlights. Knights of the road one and all, any fan on four wheels will be happy to assist a struggling fellow traveller with water for a boiling radiator or a pair of stockings for a make-do-and-mend fan belt.

So pack up your primus stove for a brew on a grass verge, stream your knitted scarf out of the back window, and set your waving-hand novelty boinging in the back window.

Happy motoring to one and all!

Back to a time when motoring away used to be a real expedition.

Candy Man:
The cool 'Pool
alternative to
nodding dogs
and furry dice.

LIVERPOOL AND

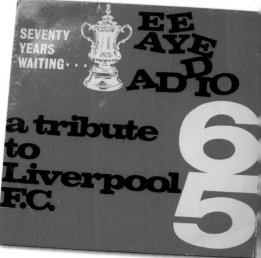

MERSEYBEAT

It's thought that football chants as we now know them originated at Anfield in the early Sixties. There were club anthems sung in the 1950s such as 'I'm Forever Blowing Bubbles' at West Ham, and 'Keep Right on to the End of the Road' at Birmingham, but Liverpool was the focus of the nation's youth in 1963 with the Beatles fronting the Merseybeat movement, and their fans take the credit for introducing a new way for football fans to support their team.

Bertie Mee said to Bill Shankly, "Have you heard of the North Bank, Highbury?"

The Sound of '66: Merseybeat band The Condors' tribute to the Reds winning the League and Everton winning the Cup.

There's grainy black-and-white footage of the Kop singing 'She Loves You', and they came up with the enduring anthem 'You'll Never Walk Alone', borrowed from Gerry & The Pacemakers, via Rodgers & Hammerstein. There's an additional theory that the synchronised clapping that became an important feature of football chants was influenced by the Brazilian fans at the 1962 World Cup in Chile, which was the first to be broadcast into British homes.

By the mid-Sixties, football songs were firmly established at just about every ground in the country. The rest of the world always eventually catches up with the Liverpool lead.

Shanks said, "No, I don't think so, but I've heard of the Liverpool Boot Boys!"

Into the Seventies, Liverpool were still the Kop Kings and their influence remained strong. In addition to 'You'll Never Walk Alone' (with accompanying scarf display), two other Anfield Anthems were blatantly nicked and adapted by 'choirs' up and down the land – one about Bertie Mee and Bill Shanklee, the other:

"We'll fight with no surrender,
We'll fight for the boys in red,
We'll fight the fight for Liverpool,
The team Bill Shankly bred."

The new Glam Rock genre with acts like T.Rex, Sweet and (whisper it) Gary Glitter, fitted perfectly with the dangerous mood on the terraces. 'Hello Hello I'm Back Again' provided the hook for one popular war cry; but then so did Tim Rice & Andrew Lloyd Webber's 'Jesus Christ Superstar'.

FERRY 'CROSS THE MERSEY

HILLSBOROUGH

As the Seventies drew to a close, revivalist mods and skinheads replaced boot boys on the Kop; but, whatever the tribe, the chants and songs remained remarkably constant. With old songs being used for decades and new ones being constantly added, the repertoire was becoming enormous.

Strange how the fans never adopted the coolest-ever football 45 as an Eighties anthem.

"You two scousers are always yapping
I'm gonna show you some serious rapping
I come from Jamaica, my name is John Barnes
When I do my thing the crowd go bananas..."

Or possibly not, when you take a cool retrospective look at the brilliant John Barnes-led 'Anfield Rap' of 1988, which brought a new wave of Merseybeatbox to the nation, as Liverpool single-handedly invented hip-hop!

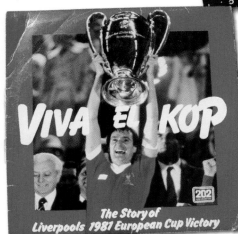

COLOUR ME BAD

Back in the day, I spent many hours scribbling away at the coarse paper of Caversham's Football Colouring Book, tongue lolling out to one side in sheer concentration, transforming the black outlines into lifelike and vibrant living colour. As you can see, I hardly ever went over the lines and had an almost eerie command of every stroke.

West Ham's brilliant puce and cyan, Everton's ultramarine, Liverpool's scarlet, Manchester City's forget-me-not blue (achieved by pressing not quite so hard on the ultramarine) were all portrayed to perfection under my artistic spell, now brought to life before your very eyes in a spectral rhapsody.

Just one tiny problem to prick my dreamlike bubble: "WHO'S GOT FELT PEN ON THE CARPET?!"

SUPER 8

For years, nearly every issue of *Shoot!* carried an advert by 'Quality Products (Romford) Ltd' (how very reassuring) for a range of 'Soccer Films' in the 8mm home-movie format.

Sadly this was a page for perusing and wishing, rather than buying, as the films were viciously expensive, given a mid-Seventies pocket-money budget.

For the unimaginable privilege of being able to watch 200 feet of the 1971 FA Cup Final WHENEVER YOU WANTED in colour, you had to lay out £10.45 in the Eighties. Which is more

Super 8 film: imagine a DVD printed out on a long strand of tinsel.

For the privilege of being able to watch 200 feet of the 1971 FA Cup Final, you had to lay out a tenner (or £3,456 in today's money).

than I paid for a season highlights DVD nearly 40 years on.

So, although we did actually own a movie projector, all I could watch on it were the two reels that we inherited with it: selected scenes from *Cowboy* starring Glenn Ford and Jack Lemmon, and an episode of *Top Cat* – both silent with subtitles.

It didn't stop me reading down the list and yearning, though: 1970 World Cup Final Brazil 4-1 Italy 200 feet – black and white... your Dad would have to have been the chairman of ICI to build up a whole library of classic games.

Somebody hurry up and invent YouTube, for Christ's sake.

SOUVENIR SHOP

Be sure and visit the LFC Megastore
the next time you drop by the ground.
That way, you can walk out of the
deal with an attractive calendar of the
playing staff as of last July (which was
out of date by the start of the season),
a corporate badged grooming set
(eyebrow notcher; beard sculptor; hair,
shower and lubricant gel) or a bargain
black nylon T-shirt worth 3 quid (today,
all third kits are either black or grey.
Why? Because they 'look good with
jeans' according to the PR man. But
hey, all sizes other than XXL and

Available at the
SOUVENIR SHOP . . .

An ideal
gift for
Xmas

ANFIELD LIVERPOOL

● **Self-assembly model of Anfield**
Price £4.95

XXXL are reduced to
a mere 30 quid! Which
is to say, 50 quid to
you.)

There's a lot
more going on at
every Premier League
ground than kicking a
ball around these days.
We're talking delights
such as business-class
banqueting, stadium
tours, a hotel with
rooms overlooking
the pitch, a members-
only gym, conference
facilities and unlimited
retail opportunities.

Bring back the old
souvenir shop, where
they only sold plastic
caps, sew-on patches and
programme binders.
None of your new-fangled
showy stuff like mugs,
mind. And no need for
bobble hats, because
that's what grans were for.

What price the return
of the half-price back-issue
programme box?

LIVERPOOL F.C.

LIVERPOOL FC
SUPPORTERS ALL OVER THE WORLD

SOUVENIR SHOP

TOPPS

For anybody who had an American penpal in the 70s, a deep feeling of jealousy always used to accompany the arrival of the aid packages from the Land of the Free, the home of rock 'n' roll, Scooby-Doo, Starsky and Hutch.

We used to send them our unwanted football card and sticker swaps – relatively drab affairs, with baldies kneeling in mud – and by return of post four months later came the most exotic, colourful, glam-rocktastic American football and baseball cards featuring unheard-of megastars with superhero uniforms and names like Ars Blagstrom, Jessie-Bob Jehosephat and Hunk Pfunk.

Then, one day in downtown 1975, poor old A&BC footer cards went bust and were eaten up by US bubble-gum barons Topps.

Almost overnight, our cards grew more exciting, sprouting multi-colours and curlicues originally designed

Back-from-the-dead stars with Captain Kirk beer guts dressed like Evel Knievel.

to surround the all-thrusting quarterbacks.

Then the NASL was promoted big in our football comics – a festival of fun with relaxed offside rules and shoot-outs, cheerleaders and players with Captain Kirk beer guts dressed like Evel Knievel. Back-from-the-dead stars played on pitches of lime-green carpet set in towering Space Age kickerdomes.

In America, they played perky organ music when the home team were in possession, and doomy chords when the baddies had the ball. In America they scored six points for a win, not a chiselling two – plus a point per goal scored up to a maximum of three.

But our cool penpals never went as far as inviting us over, did they?

Pub Quiz: Phil was a Red from 1968-75, but not a lot of fans could name his other three League teams: Boro, Luton and Swansea.

am City
ded 1875.
3, 1921, 48, 55.
Cup 1963.
yal blue

Blackburn Rovers
Founded 1874
Div 1 1912, 14.
Div 2 1939, FA Cup 1884,
85, 86, 90, 91, 1928.
Blue & white

Blackpool
Founded 1887
Div 2 1930.
Div 1 runners-up 1956.
FA Cup 1953.
Tangerine & white

Bolton Wanderers
Founded 1874.
Div 2 1909.
FA Cup 1923, 26, 29, 58.
All white

Bradford City
Founded 1903.
Div 2 1908.
Div 3 (N) 1929.
FA Cup 1911.
Claret & amber

Brighton & Hove Albion
Founded 1900.
Div 3 (S) 1958.
Div 4 1965.
Blue & white

Bristol City
Founded 1894.
Div 2 1906.
Div 3 (S) 1923, 27, 55.
All red

Bristol Rovers
Founded 1883.
Div 3 (S) 1953.
Sky blue & white

Burnley
Founded 1881.
Div 1 1921, 60. Div 2 1898.
FA Cup 1914.
English 1947, 6.
Claret, blue & w.

Everton
1878. Div 1 1891.
8, 32, 39, 63, 70.
Div 2 1931.
p 1906, 33, 66.
lue & white

Falkirk
Founded 1876.
Sc Div 2 1936, 70.
Sc Cup 1913, 57.
Navy blue & white

Football Club Badges

The Esso collection of 76 famous football club badges.
When you've completed this card you'll have a permanent record of the most famous
football clubs in England, Northern Ireland, Scotland and Wales represented
by their unique and colourful insignias. Keep it safe - you will own what may become
a valuable collector's item.

EC European Cup ECWC European Cup Winners' Cup EFC European Fairs Cup FL Football League Sc Scottish SLC Scottish League Cup

Manchester City
ded 1894. Div 1 1937,
v 2 1899, 1903, 10.
7, 66. FA Cup 1904,
6, 69. FL Cup 1970.
3 1970. Blue & white

Manchester United
Founded 1878. Div 1 1908,
11, 52, 56, 57, 65, 67.
Div 2 1936. FA Cup 1909.
48, 63. EC 1968.
Red & white

Sheffield United
Founded 1889.
Div 1 1898
Div 2 1953.
Cup 1899, 1902, 15, 25
Red, white & black

Sheffield Wednesday
Founded 1867. Div 1 1903,
04, 29, 30. Div 2 1900
26, 52, 56, 59.
FA Cup 1896, 1907, 35.
Blue & white

Shrewsbury Town
Founded 1886.
Elected to League 1950.
Welsh Cup twice.
All blue

Southampton
Founded 1885.
Div 3 (S) 1922.
Di..... 1960.
Red...

Stoke City
Fou..... 1963.
Div..... 63.
Div.....

Sunderland
Founded 1879.
Div 1 1892, 93, 95,
1902, 13, 36.
FA Cup 1937.
Red & white

Swansea City
Founded 1911.
Welsh Cup 5 times.
Div 2 (S) 1925, 49.
White & black

Swindon Town
Founded 1881
FL Cup 1969.
Dis 3 runners-up 19...
Red & white

ESSO CLUB BADGES

What was your favourite set of freebies given away with petrol back in the day? Nowadays, it's hard to imagine anything but a form for a mortgage being handed out by the garage man, as it costs the same now to fill your tank as it did to buy your first car. But this hasn't always been the case.

While the likes of Texaco and Shell seemed obsessed with making huge amounts of money by flogging us the world's overflowing natural resources, back in 1971 good old Esso were only concerned with making sure that small boys had plenty of great football stuff to collect. First, there were World Cup coins, then 'Squelchers', a series of little booklets so named because the info contained in them was enough to squelch any argument. There were FA Cup Winners coins, and the Top

STRIKER

My mate Steve and I would have the same heated debate over and over about the various merits of Subbuteo versus those of Palitoy's Striker.

Steve maintained that Striker was a far superior game, "because the players actually kicked the ball." And Subbuteo was "too fussy."

I would counter that Subbuteo didn't need a gimmick because it was virtually a sport in its own right. Striker was "only five-a-side" and its players' zones robbed you of the opportunity for a full-blooded clogger's tackle.

That's not to say there weren't Striker injuries. In fact there were two: the broken ankle or the broken neck, both incurred when you pressed a player's head down too hard.

But then Striker introduced the magnificent new goalie, cleverly geared to fling out his arms in a full-length dive when moved to the side.

Er, who's better, Steve – the Jam or the Clash?

Team Collection of Photo-Discs built a squad of Britain's best players... but best of all was surely the literally titled 'Esso Collection of Football Club Badges'.

Esso even provided a splendid fold-out presentation card to stick them in and, frankly, if there was anything more exciting happening in 1971, we can't remember it now. It wasn't just the 20p blackmail job for the 'Starter Pack' of 26 otherwise unobtainable badges that made the heart beat faster. The little foil badges were irresistible. Everyone was collecting them.

Have you still got yours?

MAKE THE BALL DO WHAT **YOU** WANT WITH

STRIKER

THE **FAST** ACTION FOOTBALL GAME WITH A KICK!

CHARITY SHIELD

Since 1908 the Charity Shield had been treated like a mixed metaphor of dog's dinner and moveable feast. Touring all the big grounds from Highbury to Goodison, it eventually settled on a formula of League Champions vs. FA Cup Winners.

However, by the early Seventies, its stock was pretty low.

In 1973 it should have been contested by Sunderland and Liverpool, but neither could be bothered, so holders Manchester City played Second Division champions Burnley at Maine Road.

When neither Liverpool nor Leeds showed much enthusiasm in fulfilling the fixture the following year, the FA decided to elevate its kudos by staging it at Wembley.

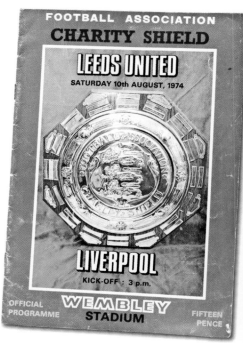

The FA decided to elevate the Charity Shield's kudos by staging it at Wembley.

They probably soon wished they hadn't, as a dirty game descended into fisticuffs with Billy Bremner and Kevin Keegan becoming the joint first British players to be dismissed under the Twin Towers, both throwing off their shirts on the way to the tunnel.

As far as the FA were concerned, this was neither charitable nor the ideal curtain-raiser to the new season, and both players were handed eleven-game suspensions.

For the rest of us, it was fantastic stuff, the only one we can remember, and certainly the only Charity Shield ever to feature in a film.

One apiece at full time, it was one of the first penalty shoot-outs many fans had ever witnessed.

Remember who scored for Liverpool, who didn't miss a single kick? In order, it was Alec Lindsay, Emlyn Hughes, Brian Hall, Tommy Smith, Peter Cormack, with Ian Callaghan the first taker to venture into the scary land of sudden death.

At which point David Harvey, the Leeds goalie, was nominated to follow in his tracks…

Sweet charity: Bremner vs. Keegan, Wembley 1974.

All you need is an Adidas bag
(with 'all day I dream about sex' added in felt pen).

BAG TAG

During our time at secondary school we invented a game that was so good we were convinced it would be adopted by every twelve-year-old boy in the land, sweeping across Britain like a forest fire; but somehow it didn't.

All you needed to make dinner-hour a time of high-octane excitement was a tennis ball. The rest of the equipment you already lugged round with you all day. Your bag.

Whether the cheapo variety with 'Sports' printed on the side; or a pricier 'Adidas' bag (with 'all day I dream about sex' added in felt pen) we placed them in a circle, the size of which was

determined by the number of players. The rules were simple, as indeed were we. You could only touch the ball with your feet. Your bag was your own individual goal. If the ball hit your bag you had one life left – a second hit and you were out of the game. You had to strike a balance between defending your own bag and forming alliances to attack someone else's. There was plenty of scope for subterfuge and double bluff and just as in *Macbeth* (which we would be studying later that day in English), overreaching ambition could swiftly lead to your downfall.

ACTION TRANSFERS

This is easy. All you have to do is scribble the transfers off their greaseproof-paper backing on to the empty pitch in front of the Kop, and soon you'll have an action-packed Instant Picture™ of a match as good as anything a photographer could produce.

Now then. Let's 'peel away backing paper' and kick off with one of the White-

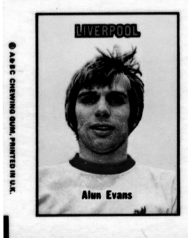

LIVERPOOL

Alun Evans

The full glory of the transfer isn't captured
until they're artistically applied to a scene...

Complete this scene using some of your instant pictures

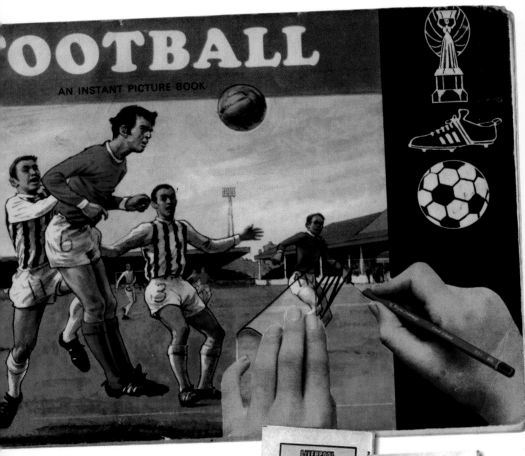

OOTBALL

AN INSTANT PICTURE BOOK

and-Violet team realistically booting the ball upfield. While his goalie jumps around out of his area. And one of the Turquoises throws a dummy on the edge of the box. While another one goes for a diving header sitting on his team-mate's shoulders.

It's no use the Letraset bods flagging up the deadly danger of failing to 'slide backing paper under other pictures to avoid accidental transfer' – it's already too late for the centre-forward's head. What we really need is more players just hanging around, like in real life, gossing and blowing on their hands and doing leg stretches...

"Tommy Smith wasn't born, he was quarried." – Bill Shankly

We shall not,
we shall not sit down,
We shall not,
we shall not sit down,
We are the KOP,
We are The Famous Spion Kop
and we shall not sit down.

We are the famous kopites

THE KOP

Anfield's new terraced end on the
Walton Breck Road was unofficially
dubbed 'Spion Kop' almost as soon as it
was opened in 1906.

    The Boer term for 'Lookout Hill'
had entered the nation's consciouness
following a Boer War battle in 1900
which had seen many
British casualties,
many from Liverpool.
Although Anfield's
wasn't the first Spion
Kop, that was at
Woolwich Arsenal's
ground in Plumstead,
it is beyond doubt that
it became the most
famous.

    In 1976 Ian St
John wrote in the
*Park Drive Book of
Football*: "... such
is the fantastic
inspiration we
Liverpool players
derive from the
Kop - the section of the
ground which contains the most
talked-about set of soccer fans in
Britain.

    "During the last six seasons
we have won nearly every major
honour the game can offer, and
I firmly believe that the Anfield
supporters can take some of the
credit for our success."

Yer real actual:
A chunk of the
Kop, hewn
from the great
concrete hill.

A HALLMARK FOOTBALL SPECIAL

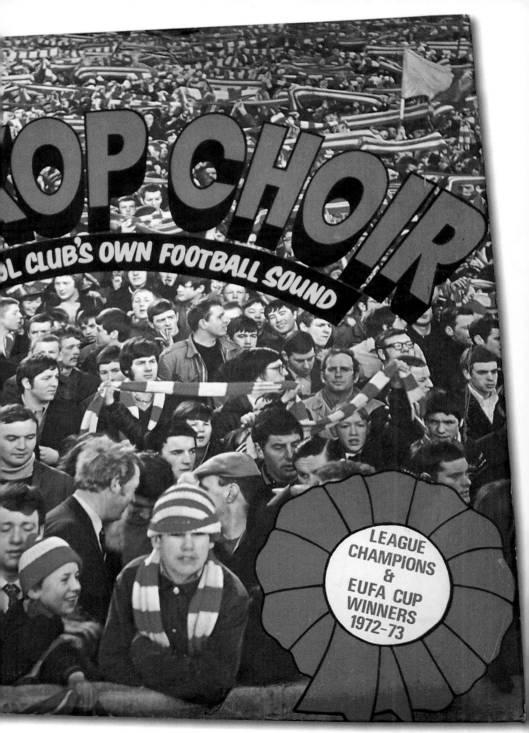

KOP CHOIR

...OL CLUB'S OWN FOOTBALL SOUND

LEAGUE
CHAMPIONS
&
EUFA CUP
WINNERS
1972-73

You may be surprised to discover that when we tracked down Gordon Milne, inside-right for Liverpool in the 60s, he revealed a glimpse of the boyish enthusiasm for the game that Bill Shankly never lost – and also the passion he shared with the followers of his Reds.

"We'd played at Brighton and come back on the train to Euston to get the train to Liverpool," Milne told us. "It was about 7 o'clock at night, there were a lot of Liverpool fans around and they'd found a deserted bit of platform to get an eight-a-side game going. Shanks joined in and there he was, tearing up and down with them for twenty minutes. You know, he didn't drink, so he couldn't just sit and have a beer, he couldn't stand still for long so there he was playing football, and that sort of thing created a very strong bond between him and the fans."

Shankly owed his clean-living lifestyle to his father who was an athlete and fitness enthusiast who never smoked or drank.

"When I go son," he once told Emlyn Hughes, "I'm going to be the fittest man ever to die."

And what about fitness for purpose, and the legendary philosophical underpinning of Shanks's system?"We devised a system of play which minimised the risk of injuries," he once claimed.

"The team played in sections of the field, like a relay. We didn't want players running the length of the field, stretching themselves unnecessarily, so our back men played in one area, and then passed on to the midfield men in their area, and so on to the front men. Whilst there was always room for individuals within our system, the work was shared out."

Hats off to us lot, Paris 1981

Alan Kennedy, goalscorer against Madrid.
And our Phil... just one of his 16 major honours

IN THE PINK

This same ritual went on up and down the country for decades, little kids and old blokes queuing up outside the paper shop at 6 o'clock on Saturday night, waiting for the sports final edition of the local paper – the *Green 'Un*, the *Pink 'Uns*, the *Blue 'Un* or the *Buff*. Any colour as long as it wasn't white. Here was sports journalism at its most demanding, where reports were phoned in on the hoof, assumptions were made before the final whistle, and last-minute goals were any editor's nightmare.

The *Pink 'Un* gave you the chance to settle down in a favourite armchair, to check the pools and peruse the results and league tables at your leisure. In the days before Sky News and even Ceefax, it was either this or wait for the arrival of the Sunday papers.

Gradually, the need for a Saturday evening sports edition lessened and then disappeared altogether. The internet was one blow – suddenly you didn't need to be standing out on the street in January – but the killer was the spreading of fixtures over the weekend due to the demands of TV.

One by one, the sports papers had to admit defeat and hold up their

The *Football Echo* match report
was vital reading
if you'd just left Anfield 80 minutes ago.

The *Football Echo* was vital reading for those fans who couldn't rest until they had read a report of a game that some of them had seen eighty minutes ago (unless they were after confirmation of a result they'd just heard played out on the radio).

hands in surrender, in Manchester and Leeds, Leicester and Coventry and Birmingham... although the Norwich *Pink 'Un* and Ipswich's *Green 'Un* are both websites now.

If you can't beat 'em, join 'em.

UP FOR THE CUPPA

In the season before the 1966 World
Cup, those nice people at Ty-Phoo Tea
were running a smashing offer whereby
any thirsty fan could collect up packet
tops and send off for a large 10" by 8"
teamgroup card of their choice.

And sometimes you'd even get a little
picture of a player printed on the side
of the box, which kids would inevitably
hack out with scissors almost before mum
could get the tea (note, that's 'tea', not
your common-as-muck not-yet-invented
'teabags') into the tea canister.

Nice cup of Rosie Lee with your eggy
soldiers in the morning? And a nice little
Roger on the side of the packet, with your
triangular toast in a little metal stand to
make it go cold extra quick...

LIVERPOOL F.C.

ROGER HUNT
(Liverpool and England)

IAN ST JOHN
(Liverpool and Scotland)

MEN ONLY

Back in the day, real men used to carry all sorts of smashing stuff around in their pockets along with their Reds season ticket in its real leather holder, so vital to prevent the harsh touch of paper on the inside of the gent's pocket.

You were no one without a handy length of string (now sneered upon as a throwback to the suspicious, militaristic Scout movement), a set of Liverpool FC darts (now banned from everywhere except the board on the back of the kitchen door), a Watney's Party Seven can opener ("puncture

both sides to ensure even flow"), and two shillings and fivepence in assorted, unfamiliar coinage ("Dad, what's a 'farting'?").

Throwing your concertina LFC-star keyring into the fruitbowl at Swinging Sixties wife-swapping parties must have guaranteed the attention of many a lady with ironed hair and/or groovy hotpants.

It was the way you used to part your long greasy hair so alluringly with your special Reds comb – and the way you used to lean on the bar and resheath the offensive weapon so thoughtfully, so meaningfully – that always used to get the Liver Birds going.

At least until they clapped eyes on your supercool LIVERPOOL RULE OK belt.

Is that an LFC comb, key ring and darts case in your pocket?
Or are you just pleased to see me?

LOWER-LEAGUE SIGNINGS

These days you'll seldom find a top club taking a punt on a lower-league signing. There are few potential stars left to be discovered as the Premier League scouting systems are as tight and effective as a purse seine tuna-fishing net: hardly anything of value can slip through the holes.

A few decades back, however, any chief scout worth his trilby knew how to sniff out a bargain from the basement level or below.

Of all these football sages, Geoff Twentyman, chief scout at Liverpool, had perhaps the best track record, recommending the signings of Kevin Keegan and Ray Clemence from Scunthorpe United; John Toshack from Cardiff City; University of Warwick student Steve Heighway, playing for Skelmersdale United; Northampton Town's Phil Neal; Alan Hansen from Partick Thistle, and Chester's Ian Rush. The Reds paid £200,000 for Rush, or £578 for each of his 346 goals, and also made £500,000 profit from farming him out to Juventus for a season.

What a steal when Watford lined up a swap deal with Sudbury Court in 1981. The signature of John Barnes had set back Graham Taylor's Hornets just one set of first-team kit. Six years later they sold him on to Liverpool for £900,000.

The Reds never had to shell out like that when Geoff Twentyman was on the case.

GOSH IT'S TOSH

While many a recently retired footballer will now employ a fawning hack to transcribe his tales of squandering millions of pounds of our money on cocaine, cars and country manors, you tend not to get so many soccer-star poets these days.

It all started when Liverpool centre-forward John Toshack nodded in a goal and made up a little rhyme about it for the local Liverpool press men.

Now, everyone in football enjoys a new tradition, especially when it fills column inches without the need for anyone to engage their brain...

Published by Duckworth in 1976, *Gosh It's Tosh* featured not only the Welsh hitman's innermost thoughts in the form of approximately rhyming doggerel, but also a series of pictures of Tosh with his classic 'little 'n' large' strike partner Kevvy Keedle – first

"We went straight at them from the start,
Their whole defence was ripped apart.
Our pre-match plans went to the letter,
Has any Liverpool team played better???"

Tosh – 'A Goalden Night'

> **We're flying off to sunny Spain. The players will be apprehensive,**
>
> # But Liverpool!
> **We won't play defensive.**

Tosh – 'Barcelona Here We Come'

dressed up as Batman and Robin, then as Edwardian gents, as Spanish bullfighters and escaped convicts. As such, it's something of a rarity.

In case you have a first (and only) edition foxing elegantly on your spare-room bookshelves, the value of a slightly dog-eared copy ('for insurance purposes', as they say on *The Antiques Roadshow*) is anything up to £1.20.

> **Something must be done and quick,**
>
> # Bob Paisley plays a master trick.
>
> **Discarding height and going for pace, He pulls me off and puts on Case.**

Tosh – 'Battle with Bruges'

HOT LEG

The black-and-white film documentary of Anfield's Kopites lustily knocking out the hits of the Beatles and Gerry & the Pacemakers in the early Sixties didn't quite tell the full story. There was a steamier side to the Kop.

A more appropriate song might have been 'Yellow River' by Christie (see 'Cowpats for Goalposts').

You see, the Kop had always suffered from a chronic lack of gangways. Once you were installed in there, then that was pretty much it. You weren't going anywhere.

If you'd spent pre-match in the alehouse then, unless you had an iron bladder, you were going to be struggling by half-time.

The solution was to roll up a newspaper or matchday programme to preserve the modesty of your little Kopite, and off he would go, right where you stood.

Your accuracy in this delicate matter was measured by whether any of your neighbours – or maybe how many – suffered what was known on Merseyside as a 'Hot Leg'.

Okay, this is something we aren't seriously suggesting bringing back.

Tube strike: beware of the bloke with a rolled-up prog and a relieved expression.

No1

£500,000
Bruce Grobbelaar

Bruce Grobbelaar

LIVERPOOL

FACTIX™
Zimbabwe keeper who transferred
from Vancouver Whitecaps in 1981.
He is extremely agile with amazing
reflexes.

No4

£450,000
Nigel Spackman

Nigel Spackman

LIVERPOOL

FACTIX™
Determined player with a whole-
hearted attitude. Signed by Chelsea
from Bournemouth for £30,000 and
transferred in 1986 to Anfield.

No5

£700,000
Ronnie Whelan

Ronnie Whelan

LIVERPOOL

FACTIX™
Dubliner Ronnie plays in the
"lucky" No 5 shirt. He's a sports
fanatic who also plays snooker,
darts and golf.

NORWICH CITY
'THE CANARIES'

n Brown

for Received: £1,000,000 from Man City
ves '80 & from Nottingham Forest
any '81
r Paid: £300,000 to Hajduk Split for
'80

= 25,500

ce: 43,984 v Leicester FA Cup 6th Rnd.

LIVERPOOL
'REDS or POOL'

FACTIX™
Manager: Kenny Dalglish
Record Transfer Received: £3,200,000 from Juventus
for Ian Rush '86
Record Transfer Paid: £900,000 to Brighton for Mark
Lawrenson '81
Ground Capacity: 45,600
Record Attendance: 61,905 v Wolves FA Cup 4th Round
1952

**SHEFFIELD
WEDNESDAY**
'THE OWLS'

FACTIX™
Manager: Howard Wilkinson
Record Transfer Received: £200,000
Gary Bannister '84
Record Transfer Paid: £266,000 to
Stainrod '85
Ground Capacity: 50,174
Record Attendance: 72,841 v Ma
5th Rnd. 1934

**TOTTENHAM
HOTSPUR**
'SPURS'

No2

£700,000
Mark Lawrenson

Mark Lawrenson

LIVERPOOL

FACTIX™
Qualified for Eire through parentage
although he was born and began his
career in Preston. One of Britain's
most accomplished defenders.

TEAMTACTIX

Well done, Pal,
You've become the proud owner of one of the best board games that I've ever
played. Teamtactix™ is fast moving, action packed and fun, and lets you
become part of the real-life dramas of a top-class football team manager…

So runs the letter from Emlyn Hughes
OBE which accompanies this big
board game box, admirably packed
with a plush fold-out board, millions
of pounds worth of hard cash,
hundreds of bang up-to-date (well,
they were in 1986) player cards
from all the top teams, a sexy little
spinner and four big Scrabble-type
racks to stretch your team out on.

At this point, it's probably
worth considering whether
Emlyn was a neutral observer of
all these shenanigans. The game
now needs a degree of analysis
to ensure it can stand the test
of the Trade Descriptions Act (1997) or

we might get into all sorts of Health &
Safety trouble for featuring it here.

Firstly, when Emlyn congratulates
you as his 'Pal', could that possibly
be because your mum or your auntie
who bought you the game has just
contributed a few bob in rake-off fees to
his Saturday night ale fund? And when
he then suggests you're proud to own
the game, could that be more of an
assumption on his part than a hard fact?

When Emlyn states that
Teamtactix™ is "one of the best board
games I have ever played," any potential
purchaser should perhaps take into
consideration the objectivity of this
apparently heartfelt recommendation.

N°6

Alan Hansen
LIVERPOOL
£650,000
Alan Hansen

FACTIX™
Alloa-born Alan is a gifted sportsman, who has represented Scotland at differing levels in various sports – including soccer.

N°7

Paul Walsh
LIVERPOOL
£800,000
Paul Walsh

FACTIX™
...via Luton...
despite...

N°8

Steve McMahon
LIVERPOOL
£800,000
Steve McMahon

FACTIX™
Steve was once a ball boy at Goodison but he "crossed the park" ... for his childhood idols in ... Aston Villa.

N°9

John Aldridge
LIVERPOOL
£750,000
John Aldridge

FACTIX™
Former toolmaker from Liverpool. Signed from Oxford in 1987 for a near £1,000,000 fee as a replacement for Ian Rush.

N°11

Craig Johnston
LIVERPOOL
£750,000
Craig Johnston

FACTIX™
Born in South Africa but raised in Australia and paid his own fare to come for trials with Middlesbrough. A keen photographer.

Corner **GAMBLE**

Emlyn Hughes' **TEAMTACTIX** ™

Pal,

You've become the proud owner of one of the best board games that I've ever played. Teamtactix™ is fast moving, action packed and fun, and lets you become part of the real life dramas of a top class football team manager.

TEAMTACTIX CLUB
Teamtactix club will become a forum for your comments and ideas on football and in particular the transfer market. The benefits of club membership will be:-

■ — Free regular newsletters
■ — Free competitions
■ — Exclusive Teamtactix merchandise offers
■ — Regularly updated player cards available only through the Club Shop.

Membership is free, just complete the form printed below and I'll send you details of the first Teamtactix Competition.

Yours

[signature]

Emlyn Hughes O.B.E.

- -

Please return to:
Teamtactix Club
PO Box 100, Gravesend, Kent DA11 0QW

Name.. Date of Birth.....................
Address...
....
Favourite Team....................................... Favourite Player.................
NOTE: Overseas Membership: £3.00 per annum to cover postage.

Emlyn suggests that the board game is "fast-moving" and "action-packed" – two compound adjective descriptions which we've certainly never heard applied to any other board game in the history of bored children on Sunday afternoons in the 1980s. As for "fun", again the definition is open-ended. Some grown men like to dress in ladies' pants and be spanked mercilessly by their real owners for "fun". Others collect stamps.

Then there's the issue of whether Teamtactix™ really does let you "become part of the real-life dramas of a top-class football manager." To be specific, it clearly doesn't. It's the "real-life" bit that's a bit of an overstatement.

Oh, hold on. We just noticed the full title of the game. It's not just Teamtactix™, it's *Emlyn Hughes'* Teamtactix™.

What a shame no one ever played the game back in the day to find out whether it was any good or not.

BEER

Beer and fags used to be the smell of football, the fuel of football, and a large part of the joy of football.

The boozer was the key venue before the match and after the match, the prime arena for the big build-up and the vital post-mortem, your time in the pub arguing about football culture only interrupted by the brief respite of a bit of fresh air at the match itself.

Bring back the boozer. Bring back the smoke lounge.
Bring on the oppo.

They don't make beer like they used to back in the day – all nice and gassy and fizzy, poured with a big scummy head as God intended, pulled into your big dimply pint pot by the modern-day miracle of electricity and a vacuum pump out of proper mass-produced barrels in the cellar. None of your rubbish lumpy so-called 'real' ale, we're talking good old Higsons Double Top and Watney's Red Barrel and the like, weak enough to drink by the gallon when it was still economically viable to visit the pub without first taking out a second mortgage to buy a round for you and half a dozen thirsty mates.

Seven pints of bitter and seven bags of scratchings to line your stomachs.
Yes sir, that'll be 72 pence, ta!

Ann Field

...mous Old Higsonians

"Seven pints of bitter and seven bags of scratchings to line your stomachs (and then the gutter four hours later). Yes sir, that'll be four pounds and 72 pence, ta."

Fact is, pubs have been miserable places to go ever since they've put a ban on the very people who used to go out on a Saturday with a sense of reckless abandon. The smokers were determined to have a good time even if it might knock 20 minutes off the tedious bed-ridden fag-end of their lives still 70 years distant. With the smokers outcast into their lean-to shelters and three-sided, room-heated hovels in the pub garden, all the sexy, smoky old atmosphere has been sucked out of the boozer – much to the joy of the few customers who want to use the snug bar as a crap restaurant, ruining the glorious smell of the beer-slopped carpets with their cheap overpriced bits of steak with blue-cheese or mustard sauce just two quid extra.

Bring back the boozer. Bring back the smoke lounge. Bring on the oppo.

ADIDAS

Taking over from Umbro in the summer of 1985, Adidas produced kits for Liverpool for 11 years up until 1995-96, at which point Reebok entered the frame. The popular German kit manufacturers came back for three more seasons in the 21st century, but as you'll now be aware, modern football is way outside the remit of this nostalgia fest!

Liverpool's first Adidas designs were simple, classy affairs with subtle self-coloured shadow-weave stripes and white shoulder/sleeve stripes that were popular not only because the League and FA Cup double was landed for the first time.

In 1989 things went a tad awry in many fans' eyes when Adidas introduced the, ahem, so-called 'birdshit kit'.

Ah well, it could've been worse: witness Arsenal's bruised banana and Manchester United's blue-and-white tablecloth of the same era.

But an even greater shock was in the pipeline for the next kit change in 1991. Perhaps as a reaction to criticism, Adidas then turned in a radical new direction. That's when they made the incredibly brave, or foolhardy, decision to drop their globally recognised trefoil logo they had used since 1972 – it was like Disney sacking the Mouse or Coca-Cola plumping for an Arial font on their cans – and launched the new Adidas Equipment three-bar logo.

They sprung multiple changes on the world in the guise of the all-new Liverpool kit (and British Racing Green away version). This featured the new three-bar logo, with large bars over the shoulder instead of stripes down the sleeves.

It sat awkwardly, all skew-wiff, across the right shoulder and the left side of the shorts for a couple of seasons, and was then shifted around to form a symmetrical pattern low on either side of the shirts and shorts from 1993 to '95.

Adidas 1986-87: the last sight of the plain Liver Bird badge, which was revamped for 1987-88 (top right).

marching orders from Anfield.

It was the end of an era which had seen three Football League championship titles, three FA Cup wins and a League Cup.

Adidas have stuck with the 'Equipment' logo ever since, the trefoil being relegated to an appearance on the heritage 'Originals' range. But it will always say 'Adidas' to us.

In 1995-96, the three-bar logo was temporarily ditched from the Reds' kit, but the very next season Adidas themselves were given their

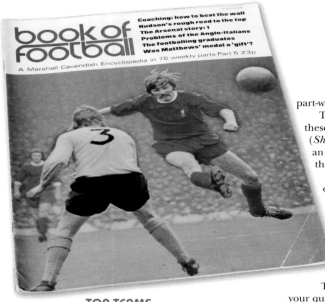

book of football

Coaching: how to beat the wall
Hudson's rough road to the top
The Arsenal story: 1
Problems of the Anglo-Italians
The footballing graduates
Was Matthews' medal a 'gift'?

A Marshall Cavendish Encyclopedia in 75 weekly parts Part 5 23p

TOP TEAMS

In 1971, the good people at Marshall Cavendish, of Old Compton Street, launched their *Book of Football*, a part-work encyclopaedia in 75 issues.

To ensure that you kept buying these weekly parts at a cool 23p (*Shoot!* was only 6p at this time) an extra incentive was nailed on to the deal.

In part two you got this 'Book of Football – Top Teams' album and each week a sheet of 16 'stickers' in random order was issued. After carefully cutting them out with the big scissors from your Mam's sewing basket they were ready to be glued in.

They had you trapped now, for your quid a month.

Only when all your Reds heroes were present and correct on their page could you relax once more.

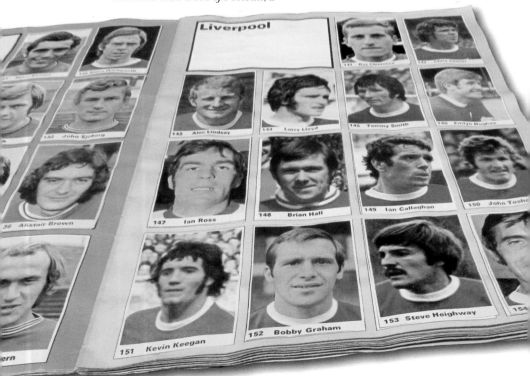

LIVERPOOL

THE OFFICIAL REVIEW OF BARCLAYS
LEAGUE DIVISION ONE · GAME BY GAME · 1988/89

CBS
FOX
VIDEO
SPORTS

THE VIDEO AGE

Seldom has a new technology flared so brightly and died so quickly as video.

The race to develop a consumer-level video system was run in 1970s Japan, with JVC and their VHS eventually managing to overshadow Sony's Betamax system, and by 1978 the first video players were available in the UK. Available, but far from affordable for all but the spoilt kids.

Most families got one some time in the middle of the Eighties. It's pretty easy to work out because that's when our magpie collections of *Match of the Day* on Kodak E-180 tapes begins – not forgetting *Saint & Greavsie* and *Football Focus* editions snagged for posterity, when the ability to capture moving pictures off the telly box still seemed like something out of *Buck Rogers in the 25th Century*.

Whether painstakingly taping goals from the regional news, or building up a video library that could be measured in yards, it was an obsessive, and ultimately a pitifully pointless exercise.

No one now plays their rare early white-label editions of black-and-white match footage from the Reds' successes in the Sixties, never mind Danny Baker's *Own Goals and Gaffs* and the endless run of season highlights from seasons that somehow now seem to all run together in the mind. They're all out in the garage now, along with the precious unplayed vinyl and the music cassettes and the slideshow projector and the magic vegetable peeler gimmicks, still mint and boxed up the same as the day you bought them from the stall on the market.

One day, the plan is to get a special machine where you link it up to your computer and convert them all into DVDs. One day.

Game by game, in real time: the video for the discerning fan with an empty week on their hands.

123

Dear Editor . . .

★ STAR LETTER

GOAL

Modestly subtitled 'The World's Greatest Soccer Weekly', *Goal* launched on 16 August 1968, with a right posh do at the Savoy with dolly birds and everything.

Its distinctive covers, with a bright yellow title on a red background and circular photo design, owed a nod to pop art, and they've stood the test of time, still looking fresh and bold to this day.

'Opinion' kicked things off – "There is no sitting on the fence with Tommy Docherty. You are either for him or very much against him" – and the long-haired Beatle-esque 'Booter' cartoon was a star turn!

There was controversy, too: a feature on ROGER HUNT, UNSUNG HERO OF THE KOP admitted he was known as a 'plodder' or 'workhorse' to his critics... needing just eight goals to beat the Reds' all-time scoring record!

Goal became a victim of its own success because exactly a year later, encouraged by decent sales, IPC introduced a second football weekly, entitled *Shoot!*

Although both went on to achieve healthy circulations of around 220,000 by 1971, *Goal* then went into decline, and its 296th and final issue came out two weeks before the start of the 1974 World Cup.

It was then 'incorporated' into *Shoot!* which was akin to having to sleep under your little brother's bed. Oh, the indignity.

GOAL
WORLD'S GREATEST SOCCER WEEKLY
1s 6d
NOVEMBER 9, 1968
No. 14

The Wels
are letting

CHARLTON'S diary . . . exclusive
ized colour . . . SHEFFIELD UNITED

GOAL
THE WORLD'S GREATEST SOCCER WEEKLY   1s 6d
SEPTEMBER 19, 1970
No. 111

BRITAIN'S
PENALTY
ACES

IAN
CALLAGHAN
Liverpool

GEORGE BEST on Irish Plans

GOAL

THE WORLD'S GREATEST SOCCER WEEKLY

JANUARY 16,
1971
No. 128
1s 6d (7½p)

Why Burnley won't go down

TOMMY
SMITH
Liverpool

MALTA SET FOR THE SLAUGHTER

GOING UP...
Fulham and Bristol Rovers

BOY SIVELL COMES IN WITH A BANG

IT'S A SIGN

Thanks go out to Lee Gray, who runs the phenomenally successful Kop Locker Facebook page, for this previously unseen picture taken back in the day – to be precise, that fateful day in 1994 when the Kop closed for business as a terrace.

Here's young Lee looking as pleased with himself as it's possible to be after witnessing the end of an era on

"I did well to get the Ladies sign
from the back wall at the top of the Kop."

the Kop, especially as the last match in front of the standing crowd was a 1-0 defeat to Norwich City.

In truth, the result was a lot less important than the emotion of the day, with Hillsborough to the fore in everyone's minds. It was a rare game when the crowd was more important than the players out on the pitch. "They did their bit," said Ian Rush of a sad, unforgettable day, "we didn't do ours."

"Everybody was looking for souvenirs, and I did well to get the Ladies sign which used to hang on the back wall at the top of the Kop," says Lee. "Out in the street after the match a bloke came up to me and offered me 20 quid for it,

but I was like, 'no way, ta.' When you think back to all the matches this sign witnessed, all the goals it's seen go in, it's an amazing feeling."

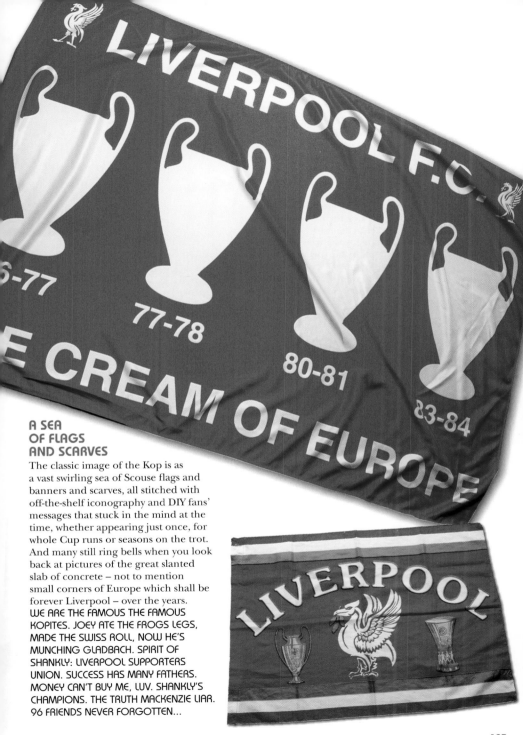

A SEA OF FLAGS AND SCARVES

The classic image of the Kop is as a vast swirling sea of Scouse flags and banners and scarves, all stitched with off-the-shelf iconography and DIY fans' messages that stuck in the mind at the time, whether appearing just once, for whole Cup runs or seasons on the trot. And many still ring bells when you look back at pictures of the great slanted slab of concrete – not to mention small corners of Europe which shall be forever Liverpool – over the years. WE ARE THE FAMOUS THE FAMOUS KOPITES. JOEY ATE THE FROGS LEGS, MADE THE SWISS ROLL, NOW HE'S MUNCHING GLADBACH. SPIRIT OF SHANKLY: LIVERPOOL SUPPORTERS UNION. SUCCESS HAS MANY FATHERS. MONEY CAN'T BUY ME, LUV. SHANKLY'S CHAMPIONS. THE TRUTH MACKENZIE LIAR. 96 FRIENDS NEVER FORGOTTEN...

TONKA

In the late 80s a disturbing trend started in the twilight world of football memorabilia collecting circles: six-inch voodoo-style representations of players from the nation's top clubs appeared on the market, produced by Tonka – Big Tough Toys for Big Tough Boys, yes? – and were ritually abused by kids twisting their trunks around at 90 degrees to their legs, turning their arms and legs at unlikely angles, and piling the little horrors up in unseemly pyramids of limbs.

They were tricky to play with, see? What else were you supposed to do with them?

Luckily for the players involved, it was always difficult to tell who was supposed to be who, so few black magic incidents and accidents were reported.

Bizarrely, we think the bland-looking hunk of plastic on the left here is Beardo. Chances are that's Barnesy and Rushy, eh? The other bod's anyone's guess.

A&BC TEAM POSTERS

We've already mentioned some of the rarities that came free with the football cards and the fossilised stick of pink bubby gum in A&BC packets back in the day.

The little team posters of 1970 vintage were one of the most popular 'little extras' at the time, and because they were so flimsy and so regularly Blu-Tacked straight on to the shrine wall, they're almost impossible to find in mint condition, and can go for silly money on eBay.

As a follow-up to the freebie extra posters (which were folded up, four times the size of a regular card), in 1973-74 A&BC tried a standalone set of bigger posters (folded up six times) – and they proved to be one of the least popular items ever released by the company.

However, for precisely that reason, if you happen to have a drawerful of old ones in mint condition, the sherbets are on you!

CHRIS LAWLER — RAY CLEMENCE — ALEC LINDSAY — TOMMY SMITH — LARRY LLOYD — EMLYN HUGHES — IAN CALLAGHAN — PETER THOMPSON — BRIAN HALL — JOHN TOSHACK — KEVIN KEEGAN — STEVE HEIGHWAY

© A&BC CHEWING GUM LTD. Ptd. in U.K.

No. 6 IN A SET OF 16.

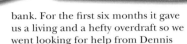

90 MINUTES

Paul Hawksbee and Dan Goldstein introduced *90 Minutes*, their new independent magazine, as 'The Serious Football Weekly' in April 1990.

Despite this well-timed launch on the eve of Italia 90, a World Cup that would re-popularise the national sport, for a while it was difficult to see where *90 Minutes* fitted among crowded newsagents' shelves alongside *Shoot!*, *Match* and *When Saturday Comes*.

Paul Hawksbee, now of Talksport radio, explained: "*90 Minutes* started life in March 1990 at 23 Charlton Road, Blackheath, London SE3. Dan Goldstein and I raised five grand through a variety of dubious sources and a further five grand from a friendly Nat West bank. For the first six months it gave us a living and a hefty overdraft so we went looking for help from Dennis Publishing who turned us around, and later IPC whose cash and clout pushed us into the Premier League."

In the IPC years *90 Minutes*, quite literally, became a red-top and developed a humorous approach to the game that was still possible when footballers could still see the joke.

It had a fanzine approach, but with a budget, and proved very popular during the *Loaded*, Brit-Pop, Newman & Baddiel era. Accordingly, the Spice Boys of Anfield, Fowler, Ruddock, Redknapp, McManaman featured regularly among features like: 'Off the Wall', 'KickBack', 'The Fools' Panel' and 'Very Much So'.

The 359th issue in May 1997 was the last. *90 Minutes* was very much for the Nineties...

PLAQUE ATTACK

Collect the Big Names Now!

And, with all due respect to Darlington and Southport, some of the smaller ones, too.

Once you'd cut out your first token from this *Shoot!* advert, ripped another off a fish-finger box and painstakingly assembled 25 new pee, then you were ready to send off and claim your embossed football club plaque from the Co-Op.

Liverpool were safely on the seemingly random list of 31 large, medium and frankly tiddler-sized clubs.

It's All at Your Co-Op... NOW!

However, somewhat oddly, these vital tribal territory markers were also presented as a Typhoo Tea promotion a year later, in the 1972-73 season, with a

EMBOSSED CLUB PLAQUES

Only 25p and 2 tokens from special Co-op packs

And getting the tokens is as easy as doing the shopping because they're on all kinds of Co-op products from cream crackers to fish-fingers. To help you get started here's your first Football Plaque Token free! Full details of where to post etc., are on all the special Co-op Football Token packs. Watch out for them. The large plaque shown here is actual size, and the full list of plaques available is:

Leeds	Wolves	Notts. Forest	Oldham
Manchester United	Birmingham	Hull	Peterborough
	West Brom.	Portsmouth	Shrewsbury
	Millwall	Coventry	Darlington
	Sheffield United	Charlton	Southport
	Newcastle	Bristol City	Stockport
City	Sheffield Wednesday	Luton	Middlesbrough
	Southampton	Lincoln	

(If your club is not listed, write to the address on Co-op label packs for further information)

YOUR FIRST ONE FREE!
(Only 1 free token accepted per plaque!)

It's All at your Co-op now!

CO OP

similar wedge of two tokens and 25p required.

A second chance to stick one firmly to the outside of your bedroom door with four foam Sellotape sticky fixers. That baby was never coming off in one piece...

The 25p plaque: from a time when 25p was 25p – or very nearly five bob.

FOOTBALL CLUB PLAQUES
1 TOKEN
25p each
plus 2 tokens

DOING PENNANTS

Curiously, it's only two classes of games at either end of the importance spectrum – big European matches and Cup Finals, and utterly meaningless friendlies – that attract the attention of the club pennant maker, who provides the skipper with a long triangle of plasticky silk hanging off a length of dowling to hand over to the oppo captain before the toss-up.

Ever was it thus, though exactly why it's impossible to say. It was something to hang in the trophy cupboard during those long barren spells, we suppose. Treasured mementoes of clammy handshakes before the hacking began.

Far more fun than the official jobbies are these cheap plastic pennants designed for children to hang on their walls with less just-pretend po-faced ceremony. It's the ones that you could buy off the market for tuppence which are now worth most to collectors. The ones with the worst-drawn images of silverware and stars, and only partially accurate lists of trophies won before you were born.

FANCY DRESS

Just when you thought we wouldn't be able to resist putting in that infamous pic of Keeg and Tosh dressed up as Batman and Robin... here's the dynamic duo again at the mercy of the tabloid snappers and an am-dram cossie department as 'sharpshooter' Robin Hood and his partner in crime, Friar Tuck.

When you consider that we could also have gone large on the famous pic of Keeg and Tosh as moustache-twiddling Edwardian gents, with cigars, boaters and stripy blazers, or any number of sombrero shots that followed the 1976 UEFA Cup semi when Toshack's goal helped the Reds beat Cruyff and Neeskens' Barca and become the first and only English side ever to win at the Nou Camp... it's enough to make you realise how tough soccer stars had it back in the 70s!

Liverpool

UMBRO

Umbro had been making fantastic football kits since 1924, when the HUMphreys BROthers Harold and Wallace set up a workshop in Wilmslow, Cheshire. In those less ostentatious days labels were worn on the inside of clothes, not the outside, so their prestigious list of classic kits remained largely anonymous.

Blackpool's famous FA Cup triumph of 1953, Tottenham's 1961 Double, England's World Cup glory in 1966, Celtic's European Cup win in Lisbon in '67 and Manchester United's the following year were all achieved in Umbro kit, with not a visible diamond in sight.

Umbro were the first to produce a full set of football kit replicas for kids in 1959, which became hugely popular when Denis Law endorsed them in the mid-Sixties.

By the time I was taken into our local sports outfitters for my first football kit, circa 1973, they were called the 'Umbroset' and came in a box with a cellophane front, affording you a tantalising glimpse of the shirt, shorts and 'hose' contained within (as they weren't interchangeable, you had to be 'average' size and keep your fingers crossed).

By 1973, branding was beginning to creep in and the little diamond logo appeared on Liverpool shirts, until, on the eve of the 1976-77 season, an advert appeared in *Shoot!* proclaiming: "It's going to be a sparkling season... just look at those diamonds!"

It's going to be a sparkling season... just look at all those diamonds!

Six years after Brazil had won the 1970 World Cup in Umbro without a single diamond showing, the new range of Umbro kits now sported dozens, with multi-logoed tape down the sleeves and shorts.

However, Liverpool resisted the trend and stuck with their plain, simple and sublime v-neck design with gold Umbro logo and badge while all around succumbed to the new designer movement. This shirt did set a precedent of its own however, becoming the first to bear an advert - 'HITACHI'. Anfield was finally breached by modern design in 1982 when the Reds adopted pinstripes and a new sponsor in 'Crown Paints' - a kit that lasted for three seasons.

Sadly, Umbro have been swallowed up, and spat out, by American giants Nike, who took over the long-running England contract.

It's probably just as well that Harold Humphreys – described as "the Dior of the football world" by the *Daily Express* in 1963 – isn't still around to witness what might be the double diamond's demise.

137

XMAS MORNING

Our 1970s Christmases, in our terrace front rooms and boxy housing-estate semis, weren't quite the same as the sumptuous Victorian festivals portrayed on Christmas cards and chocolate boxes, in TV ads and cartoons.

We didn't have stockings hanging from huge holly-bedecked fireplaces. We had striped pillowcases stuck on the end of our beds.

We didn't have gaily laughing guests – gentlemen in top hats and ladies wearing furry muffs – we had bald, moustachioed visitors in their new V-neck jumpers, and they hardly spoke.

And we had, to be frank, shite artificial Christmas trees, not those towering, richly decorated spruces portrayed on the cover of the *Radio Times*.

As for the romantic notion of a White Christmas, it never snowed round our way; though sometimes it rained.

Christmas dinner was the same as normal Sunday dinner, except with turkey instead of roast beef, and with added parsnips and sprouts. Rather than the mouthwatering spreads portrayed ... well, you get the idea.

Subbuteo accessories housed in their pale green boxes.

So we never took a horse-drawn sled down to the pine forest to chop down the tallest tree to place by the main staircase like those privileged Victorians... but then, they never had Subbuteo Team No. 41, did they?

From us to you: Have a very happy Christmas, and a splendid New Year in 1979.

We never had sleds and holly-bedecked fireplaces but, then, they never had Subbuteo Team No. 41, did they?

But somehow, on Christmas morning, with Noel Edmonds visiting children in hospital as a televisual backdrop, we still managed to reach a goosebump-inducing level of excitement.

And it was all because we knew that, concealed in cheap Woolies wrapping paper, piled up under the shite tree, there lurked *Shoot!* annuals, Wembley Trophy footballs, full football strips and

JUSTICE FOR THE 96

Respectfully dedicated to the memory of the 96 people who tragically lost their lives due to the events at Hillsborough on 15 April 1989.

John Alfred Anderson (62)
Colin Mark Ashcroft (19)
James Gary Aspinall (18)
Kester Roger Marcus Ball (16)
Gerard Bernard Patrick Baron (67)
Simon Bell (17)
Barry Sidney Bennett (26)
David John Benson (22)
David William Birtle (22)
Tony Bland (22)
Paul David Brady (21)
Andrew Mark Brookes (26)
Carl Brown (18)
David Steven Brown (25)
Henry Thomas Burke (47)
Peter Andrew Burkett (24)
Paul William Carlile (19)
Raymond Thomas Chapman (50)
Gary Christopher Church (19)
Joseph Clark (29)
Paul Clark (18)
Gary Collins (22)
Stephen Paul Copoc (20)
Tracey Elizabeth Cox (23)
James Philip Delaney (19)
Christopher Barry Devonside (18)
Christopher Edwards (29)
Vincent Michael Fitzsimmons (34)
Thomas Steven Fox (21)
Jon-Paul Gilhooley (10)
Barry Glover (27)
Ian Thomas Glover (20)
Derrick George Godwin (24)
Roy Harry Hamilton (34)
Philip Hammond (14)
Eric Hankin (33)
Gary Harrison (27)
Stephen Francis Harrison (31)
Peter Andrew Harrison (15)
David Hawley (39)
James Robert Hennessy (29)
Paul Anthony Hewitson (26)
Carl Darren Hewitt (17)
Nicholas Michael Hewitt (16)
Sarah Louise Hicks (19)
Victoria Jane Hicks (15)
Gordon Rodney Horn (20)
Arthur Horrocks (41)

Thomas Howard (39)
Thomas Anthony Howard (14)
Eric George Hughes (42)
Alan Johnston (29)
Christine Anne Jones (27)
Gary Philip Jones (18)
Richard Jones (25)
Nicholas Peter Joynes (27)
Anthony Peter Kelly (29)
Michael David Kelly (38)
Carl David Lewis (18)
David William Mather (19)
Brian Christopher Mathews (38)
Francis Joseph McAllister (27)
John McBrien (18)
Marian Hazel McCabe (21)
Joseph Daniel McCarthy (21)
Peter McDonnell (21)
Alan McGlone (28)
Keith McGrath (17)
Paul Brian Murray (14)
Lee Nicol (14)
Stephen Francis O'Neill (17)
Jonathon Owens (18)
William Roy Pemberton (23)
Carl William Rimmer (21)
David George Rimmer (38)
Graham John Roberts (24)
Steven Joseph Robinson (17)
Henry Charles Rogers (17)
Colin Andrew Hugh William Sefton (23)
Inger Shah (38)
Paula Ann Smith (26)
Adam Edward Spearritt (14)
Philip John Steele (15)
David Leonard Thomas (23)
Patrick John Thompson (35)
Peter Reuben Thompson (30)
Stuart Paul William Thompson (17)
Peter Francis Tootle (21)
Christopher James Traynor (26)
Martin Kevin Traynor (16)
Kevin Tyrrell (15)
Colin Wafer (19)
Ian David Whelan (19)
Martin Kenneth Wild (29)
Kevin Daniel Williams (15)
Graham John Wright (17)

MAY 1989 £1.20

FOOTBALL today

FOOTBALL today

Authors

Gary Silke and Derek Hammond are the authors of *The Lost World of Football* (Pitch, 2013); *What A Shot! Your Snaps of the Lost World of Football* (Pitch, 2013), and *Got, Not Got: The A-Z of Lost Football Culture, Treasures & Pleasures* (Pitch, 2011).

Picture Credits

Getty Images: Cover (Boot Room), 16, 20, 26, 34, 42, 49, 51, 54, 65, 67, 72, 106, 108, 135.
Gerard Scully: 10 (rosettes), 52 (BAB stickers), 56 (testimonial programmes).
Guy Keeley: 40, 41.
Vectis Auctions – collectible toy specialists, www.vectis.co.uk: 58 (ice-cream van), 91 (Austin Countryman).
Unofficial Liverpool Football Club Museum: 66 (rattle).
Kids in Kits, pages 76 and 77: Chris Oakley (with Ray Reardon), Lee Gray (at Wembley), Simon Kidd (with Alan Hansen), Mat and Gareth Brown, and Bryan Davin (with thanks to Rob Stokes).
Steve Marsh: 111 (packet).
Chris Andrews: 131 (plaque).

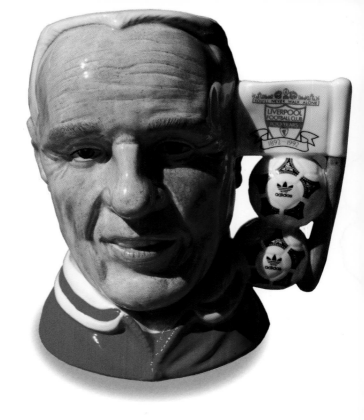

Acknowledgments

Thanks to Lee Gray, curator of the Kop Locker page on Facebook, for a huge amount of personal memorabilia – badges, flags, mugs, progs, shirts, scarves, scrapbooks, tickets, videos, pennants, bags, personal photos, records, Kop toilet sign and other memorabilia – without whom this book would not have been possible. Check out facebook.com/TheKopLocker for yet more of Lee's amazing collection.

Thanks also to Jim Donnelly at the Unofficial Liverpool Football Club Museum – facebook.com/UnofficialLFCMuseum – which is packed with thousands of historical delights.

Paul Woozley, the proprietor of the excellent oldfootballgames.co.uk website, who let us take photos of, and even play with, all his great stuff.

Nigel Mercer for his Lion league ladders, A&BC team poster and Letraset. Check out his ace, encyclopaedic football card and sticker website at cards.littleoak.com.au. And, if you're a Letraset fan, the SPLAT Archives at action-transfers.com.

Allen Brydges for letter on p.59.

Gordon Milne for our interview.

John Toshack for sundry unforgettable lines from *Gosh, It's Tosh*.

Shellie Marlowe for proof-reading.

More Critical Acclaim for *Got, Not Got*

"This exquisite book is a homage to the game of 40 years ago – not just the mudheaps and the mavericks but a celebration of its wider culture [which] rises above lazy, modern-life-is-rubbish nostalgia... The design is so sumptuous and the stories so well chosen and written that it's hard to resist the authors' conclusion that much – call it charm, character or even romance – has been lost in the rush for cash. Regardless of whether it really was a golden age, this is a golden volume, as much a social history as a sports book. If you've not got *Got, Not Got*, you've got to get it."
Backpass

"I can guarantee that virtually anybody who flicks open this magnificent book will immediately want to have it."
The Football Trader

"For further reminders of the long-lost game of the 1960s, '70s and '80s, the illuminating new book *Got, Not Got* does a very fine job."
Sport magazine

"If, like myself, you are an unashamed nostalgia junkie, this book is for you. It's more than just a book on football collectables, including memories and experiences from the golden age – a time before the FA Premiership and TV money took us through a pound-sign portal and into a parallel, but much less likeable, universe. Some of my favourite experiences/memories are included – I found myself saying either 'did it' or 'remember it' – and there's a heck of a lot to choose from."
Programme Monthly

"A huge success and an epic tome for lovers of football nostalgia everywhere."
The Football Attic blog

"It's an absolute beauty."
Adrian Goldberg, BBC Radio WM.

"An absolute gem of a book – part brilliantly written lament for an earlier age, part opportunity to reminisce about a time when you hankered after a Garden Goal ('Every Boy's Dream!')... Football's relentless commercialisation comes, naturally enough, at a cost. It's brought us everything from the Stalinist-style obliteration of the game's pre-1992 history to the modern player, kissing the badge, logo and sponsor's name after scoring. A purer, less cynical era is depicted throughout *Got, Not Got*. Buy it – you will not be disappointed."
SportsBookoftheMonth.com

"The best dose of retro football nostalgia ever. I can't put it down!"
footballcardsuk.com

"It's a beautiful book – a smorgasbord!"
John Keith, City Talk FM, Liverpool

"An exhaustively researched collection of football programmes, stickers, badges and memorabilia, a coffee table book you can dip in and out of at any time. Some of the advertisements from old programmes are classics – 'Bovril – hot favourite for the cup!' Or culinary advice to players: 'Full English – eat up your fried bread now, it's full of energy.' Eat your heart out Arsene Wenger."
Christopher Davies, Football Writers Association Book Reviews, footballwriters.co.uk

"The wonderful book *Got, Not Got* – more of the same can be found on their equally superb blog."
ThreeMatchBan.com

"It is far more enjoyable to think about football in times past, and it is a seam that is
tapped so richly by authors Derek Hammond and Gary Silke, who have written a wonderful
A to Z of lost football culture, treasure and pleasures."
The Blackpool Gazette

"A book exploring the lost culture of the game when pitches were mudbaths, managers wore
sheepskin coats and players were too embarrassed to dive - a bygone age that seems a far cry
from the profit-driven game today played in the main by overpaid primadonnas."
Paul Suart, *Birmingham Evening Mail*

"Kampprogrammer, fotballfrimarker, fotboltegneseriert... smakfullt illustrert. Just get yourself one!"
PIN magazine, Norway

"This was in WSAG's Christmas stocking and it's fantastic.
Co-written by one of our fanzine chums Gary Silke, editor of The Fox, it is an amazing collection of
half-forgotten things and much loved memories. It covers mainly the 1970s when football itself seemed
more innocent (probably only because we were all still at school back then).
But if you're the same age as us then this book has your name all over it.
Admiral kits, football Action Men, League Ladders, Esso badges. On and on we could go...
Buy it. Well worth it."
When Skies Are Grey

"Outstanding."
Miniboro.com, the Middlesbrough FC, art and interviews website

"A great read with fantastic visuals, the book reflects on how football used to be before the sanitisation
of the Premier League. Amusing and quirky, this book captures the spirit of football from the terraces.
This book is an absolute must for any footballing household."
King of the Kippax

"*Got, Not Got* is wonderful. I'm feeling quite emotional leafing through it!"
Nick Alatti, The Bridge 102.5FM in the Black Country

"In an imaginary Victorian boozer in a sepia-tinted corner of the globe, old blokes gather to talk about
football back when it was good. It is a tempting retreat, with some fantastic flagship vehicles such as
Got, Not Got and 500 Reasons To Love Football using modern media to hark back to a glorious past."
theseventytwo.com

"It would have been easy to just produce a book of nostalgic memorabilia.
It's something else to have a book that captures the heart and soul of the time.
I didn't just look back fondly, I had flashbacks full of excitement!
A wonderful journey back into our childhoods..."
God, Charlton and Punk Rock blog

"A real treat – the ideal Christmas gift for anybody who loves their retro football.
With a page dedicated to Hull City, 'Fer Ark' and all, this is the perfect football book for this time of year."
Hull City FC official website

"Whatever the football fad that accompanied the era that you got into football, you'll find it all revisited in
the wonderful book *Got, Not Got*. It's a great book, every page has a throwback memory for any football fan
over 30 and you'll dip in and out of it for months on end as I have done."
Nick Sports Junkie blog